D1561184

MESSERSCHMITT
Bf 109

Text by
ROBERT GRINSELL / Illustrations by RIKYU WATANABE

Jane's Publishing Company Limited

London • Sydney

Acknowledgements

The information contained in this book has been researched from official records, photographs, correspondence and personal contacts, but due to the span of years since the Bf 109 first took flight and the fact that several company and personal files on the Bf 109 have been destroyed, a number of assumptions and conclusions had to be made, not only by this author, but by numerous others. My conclusions are, however, not without substance, being based on the information and recall of a number of individuals and organizations whose World War II relation to the Bf 109 was one of everyday dependence.

It is to these individuals and organizations who have provided the foundation for this book, that I wish to extend my gratitude for their cooperation, trust, and friendship which have made this effort possible.

Gerhard Barkhorn	Messerschmitt-Boelkow-Blohm, G.m.b.H.
Wilhelm Batz	Guenther Rall
Adolf Galland	Royal Air Force
Gemeinschaft der Jagdflieger	Johannes Steinhoff
Erich Hartmann	United States Air Force Office of Information
Dietrich Hrabak	
Hajo Herrmann	West German Air Force
Herbert Kaiser	West German Bundesarchiv/Koblenz
Hans-Joachim Kroschinski	Walter Wolfrum

(BUNDESARCHIV)

This book was designed and produced by Wing & Anchor Press, a division of Zokeisha Publications, Ltd., 5-1-6, Roppongi, Minato-ku, Tokyo/123 East 54th Street, New York 10022.

First published in Great Britain by Jane's Publishing Company, Ltd., 238 City Road, London, EC1V 2PU.

Printed and bound in Japan.
First printing, August, 1980.

ISBN No. 0 7106 0034 8

Introduction

The Bf 109 provides history with an interesting paradox. An unwanted fighter during its early development—due to unwarranted political influence and the high risk associated with its innovative and advanced design—it was to become the standard by which all other fighters of the World War II era would be judged.

Serving the Luftwaffe in almost every capacity including interceptor, fighter-bomber, night-fighter, photo-reconnaissance, escort fighter, and ground attack, the basic Bf 109 airframe survived the duration of the European conflict as the mainstay of the German air force, being produced in a greater number than any other plane (over 30,000 were delivered) past or present. The Bf 109 was also produced in more variants than any other aircraft of its era, with over eleven variants of the G version alone.

Although the Bf 109 had a number of inherent drawbacks that at times detracted from its adaptability to its multi-mission role, with a capable pilot at its controls it was normally more than a match for any of its counterparts. Its effectiveness is attested to by the fact that from its initial flight trials in 1935 until it was finally phased out of service with the Spanish Air Force in 1967, the basic Bf 109s career spanned over 30 years with various countries around the world.

Background

In 1940, some five years after its first introduction, the now famous Bf 109 remained superior to any fighter aircraft of the time. In 1945, with the ending of hostilities in Europe, the Bf 109 was still considered to be a more than formidable enemy in the hands of a competent pilot. The introduction of what was to become the standard dayfighter for the Luftwaffe, however, was anything but ordinary. It was, in fact, the result of a number of daring and unconventional business tactics and several fortunate twists of fate that eventually provided the Bf 109 with the opportunity it deserved to prove itself the capable and respected fighter it was to become.

One of the primary reasons for the success of the Bf 109 lay in the factors that influenced its advanced structural design and unique aerodynamic features. Although the concepts were radical for their time, the majority of them were not new, having been tried and tested on several earlier aircraft from various manufacturers around the world. It was, however, in the Bf 109 that all the concepts and aero-technological advances were married into a single aircraft. The risk of this approach was evident, but the relationship of the *Bayerische Flugzeugwerke* (Bavarian Aircraft Works) to the German government, left the company with no other alternative in the competition for a new Luftwaffe fighter.

The poor standing of the *Bayerische Flugzeugwerke* (BFW) and the *Luftwaffenfuehrungsstab* (Operations Staff) had its origin in 1929 and involved a disagreement between Dr. Willy Messerschmitt and Erhard Milch, the Director of *Lufthansa* Procurement. Messerschmitt had established his own aircraft manufacturing company, *Messerschmitt Flug-zeughbau G.m.b.H.*, in March, 1926 and, based on early successes, had been provided a subsidy from the Bavarian State Government. However, the government was also financially obligated to BFW, also formed in 1926 under the sponsorship of the Bavarian State Government, German Defense Ministry and a banking firm. It became apparent in 1927 that the Bavarian Government could not support both aircraft firms, and pressure was brought to bear on Messerschmitt to merge his company with BFW. On 8 September 1927, an agreement was signed which assigned total design and development responsibility for new aircraft to the Messerschmitt team and production responsibility to the BFW firm.

The initial aircraft to be designed and produced under this new arrangement was a 10-seat passenger plane designated M-20.

Numerous problems plagued the development schedule of the aircraft and after the first prototype crashed during flight trials in February, 1928, *Lufthansa*, represented by Erhard Milch, cancelled the order. A second prototype was quickly produced and after a successful flight test, the order was reinstated by *Lufthansa*. A year later, however, the order for 10 of the M-20s was again cancelled and *Lufthansa* requested its downpayment returned. The BFW, having utilized one portion of this funding to place long lead material and component orders, and still another portion to finance in-house development of more advanced aircraft, was unable to meet the repayment demands and filed bankruptcy on 1 June, 1931.

The heated exchanges between Messerschmitt and Milch during this period resulted in an irreversible hatred between the two men that was to last through future years and have a definite influence on the success of BFW and on the design of the Bf 109.

Under Messerschmitt's direction, the BFW was reformed and reorganized; however, the bitterness that existed between Messerschmitt and Milch, who had risen to the position of Secretary of State of Aviation under Adolf Hitler, continued to restrict growth and progress of the firm. Milch was adamant in his objective of restricting the BFW's role in support of the new government's aircraft program to strictly a licensed, second-source producer of other German aircraft manufacturer's designs.

Due to the lack of German government support, either for commercial or military aircraft projects, Messerschmitt decided to chance the punishment of the Hitler regime and to solicit business outside of Germany in an effort to maintain his small design and manufacturing team. The company was successful in obtaining a pair of contracts from Rumania which placed orders for a commercial transport and a single-seat trainer under the designations M-36 and M-37.

It took Milch only a few days to publicly denounce Messerschmitt and the BFW for their support of a foreign government's (and possible future enemy's) aircraft industry. The Gestapo made a number of visits to Augsburg to discuss the matter with Messerschmitt and other officials of the *Bayerische Flugzeugwerke*. However, the young Messerschmitt held his ground and reiterated the fact that the only means of monetary support for his fledgling firm must come from foreign countries due to the prevailing attitudes of Milch and other members of the *Reichsluftministerium* (RLM).

No further actions were taken against Messerschmitt or the BFW, most likely due to the close relationship of Hermann Goering, Minister of Aviation, and Theo Croneiss, whom Goering had personally asked to join Messerschmitt in 1933 to assist in reorganizing and rebuilding the reformed BFW.

A fortunate turn of events for the BFW finally occurred in late 1933 when the Luftwaffe decided that the 4th *Challenge de Tourisme Internationale,* taking place in 1934, would provide the new German government with an opportunity to display its advanced aviation technology. The *Bayerische Flugzeugwerke* was, along with other German aircraft producers, requested to design and develop a competition sports plane for the races. BFW had, in fact, developed an aircraft for the 1932 *Challenge de Tourisme Internationale* under the designation M-29. However, the first of the four to be built crashed on 8 August. The following day, a second plane lost power in flight and although the pilot was able to bail out, the flight mechanic was killed in the ensuing crash, and the M-29 was grounded and prohibited from participating in the races.

Due to the limited time available and the advanced state of design progress made on the Rumanian-ordered M-37 trainer, Messerschmitt decided to base the new sports plane on the M-37 airframe. By October, 1933, the BFW was machining metal for the redesignated Bf 108. The aircraft was a two-seater with side-by-side controls, and incorporated a highly advanced monoplane construction with a flush-riveted stressed outer skin. Powered by a 250 hp Hirth HM-8U in-line V-8 or a 218 hp Argus AS-17, the Bf 108A attained airspeeds in excess of 320 km/h (200 mph) and was extremely maneuverable. The small wing of the Bf 108 was fitted with both leading and trailing edge slots for maximum lift and was constructed around a single-spar concept patented by Messerschmitt.

The initial Bf 108A was flown in February, 1934, at the BFW airfield near Augsburg, and the results of the trials exceeded even the most optimistic performance projections of the BFW staff. The next five aircraft rolled off the assembly lines at Augsburg between February and June and were accepted by the Luftwaffe for competition flying by a team of expert military pilots headed by Theo Osterkamp. Although minor problems with the aircraft appeared between May and June, no major setbacks were incurred and the flight testing proceeded without any substantial delays.

Then, on 27 July 1934, the bad luck which had been a constant nemesis to Messerschmitt, appeared again. The first prototype, coded D-LBUM, crashed and killed the pilot, a member of the Ministry of Aviation. In an effort to ensure that the Bf 108 would not be grounded as had the 1932 M-20, Messerschmitt and the design staff at the BFW worked feverishly to incorporate modifications into the remaining five aircraft to preclude reoccurrence of the mishap. The plane was finally certified before the end of July and cleared to race.

The Bf 108 performed admirably, but finished behind a pair of Polish RWD-9s (RWD-6s had won the rally in 1932) and a German Fieseler Fi 97. Proving itself the fastest of the aircraft entered, however, the Bf 108 had laid the groundwork for the entry of the BFW into the Luftwaffe's pending new fighter competition and had justified the firm's belief in the new construction techniques and advanced technological concepts employed in its design.

The initial specifications for a new Luftwaffe fighter were formulated and issued in early 1934 to Focke-Wulf, Arado and Heinkel. However, due to the influence of Erhard Milch, no request was forwarded to the BFW. The new fighter was the result of studies conducted by the *C-Amt* (Technical Office) of the German Air Ministry and required a low-wing monoplane configuration with a minimum armament of a pair of 7.9-mm MG 17 machineguns and performance characteristics that emphasized structural integrity during a powered dive, spin recovery controls, and provisions for being fitted with a high performance liquid-cooled inverted V-12 cylinder powerplant. (Two companies, Junkers and Daimler-Benz, were actively engaged in the development of this powerplant at the time of the specification release by *C-Amt*).

A combination of events including the friendship of Goering and Croneiss, the respect of several Luftwaffe officers familiar with the Bf 108A and uninvolved in the Messerschmitt/Milch feud, and the workloads of the other aircraft firms, finally resulted in the issuance of a development contract to BFW in 1935 for a competitive fighter aircraft. Informed by Milch, that it was solely a development contract and that no production contract would be let to BFW, Messerschmitt was faced with a decision to accept the award and try to overcome Milch's bias with a superior aircraft, or to decline the contract, which at the time promised no long term security, and instead accept an offer for

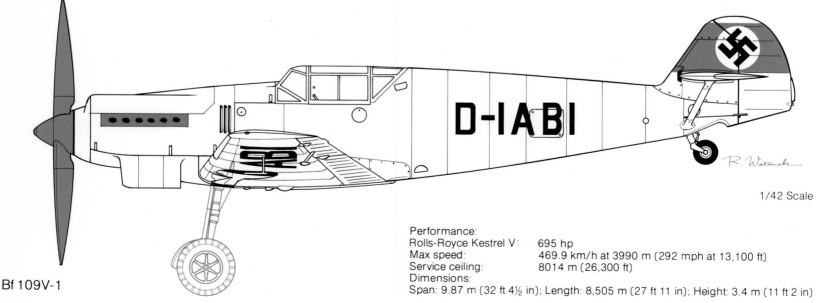

Bf 109V-1

1/42 Scale

Performance:
Rolls-Royce Kestrel V: 695 hp
Max speed: 469.9 km/h at 3990 m (292 mph at 13,100 ft)
Service ceiling: 8014 m (26,300 ft)
Dimensions:
Span: 9.87 m (32 ft 4½ in); Length: 8,505 m (27 ft 11 in); Height: 3.4 m (11 ft 2 in)

full professorship at Danzig Technical University. Fortunately for Germany, Messerschmitt opted for the former and pushed forward with his innovative and unique fighter design, the Bf 109.

Had Milch, even in his most far reaching fantasies, anticipated that the proposed Bf 109 would have even been an equal to the concepts submitted by the other firms, let alone far superior, he would surely never have approved the prototype development contract for the BFW.

The Bf 109 proposed by BFW had actually been on the drawing boards of Messerschmitt's staff since the initial flight of the Bf 108 in February, 1934, and was designed around the basic Bf 108A airframe. Like the Bf 108, the Bf 109A incorporated the cantilever low-wing monoplane configuration and retracting landing gear, and the single place cockpit was fitted with a fully hinged canopy.

The prototypes for the design were initiated in late 1934 and by August, 1935, the first of these was ready for ground trials at Augsburg. The aircraft was fitted with a Rolls-Royce Kestrel V-12 upright-vee liquid-cooled powerplant with a 695 hp rating at take-off. The Kestrel engine was used in the early prototype Heinkel He 112, Arado Ar 80 and the Bf 109 due to the lack of availability of the new Junkers Jumo 210 and Daimler-Benz DB 600 engines which were still undergoing development testing.

The trials at Augsburg, including extensive undercarriage testing on the struts and retraction, and extension mechanisms, were completed without problems. After undergoing minor modifications, the Bf 109A V1, (V designation for experimental) coded D-IABI, was flight-tested for the first time in September. Successful completion of these initial flight trials, which verified the handling characteristics and performances of the basic design, led to acceptance of the aircraft for flight testing at Rechlin (Luftwaffe Test Center). The Bf 109A V1 was flown to Rechlin and was immediately the object of suspicion by the assembled Luftwaffe test pilots. Used to the open cockpit, low wing loadings, and sturdy construction of the earlier biplanes, the test pilots could not accept the fully enclosed cockpit, innovative automatic wing slots, and the high ground angle of the new fighter which restricted the forward view during taxiing.

The exhibitions of the Bf 109As flight characteristics, including a 467 km/h (290 mph) airspeed which was 5% faster than the He 112 V1 (also at Rechlin for evaluation),

did little to overcome the test pilots' bias for the wide track, lower wing loading He 112. In the meantime, unconcerned that the He 112 was considered to be the forerunner in the fighter competition by knowledgeable Luftwaffe personnel, the BFW continued construction of the second and third prototypes. With the availability of the Junkers Jumo 210A powerplant, the second aircraft Bf 109A V2 was completed in October, 1935. The V2 differed from the V1 only in the powerplant installation, a few minor structural modifications to the undercarriage, and in the addition of an air intake for cooling of the proposed MG 17 machine-guns which would be installed in the aircraft's cowling. The fitting of the machine-guns occurred for the first time on the Bf 109A V3, and was the only change from the V2 aircraft. (The V3, however, did not roll off the Augsburg assembly line until May, 1936, due to delays in the delivery of the required Jumo 210A engine).

With the elimination of the Arado and Focke-Wulf prototypes from serious competition due to mechanical failures and low performance, the unwanted and unpopular design from the *Bayerische Flugzeugwerke* suddenly found itself in a position to become the next generation Luftwaffe fighter. Adding to the Bf 109s favor was the fact that German Intelligence had, in mid-1936, reported the production order of the new Royal Air Force Supermarine Spitfire, an aircraft much like the Messerschmitt in so far as it incorporated many similar technological advances.

In addition, continued superior performance demonstrated by the Bf 109 in comparison to the heavier and slower He 112 was beginning to influence even the most determined detractors of the BFW fighter at the RLM. As the flight evaluation trials continued through the fall of 1936 at Travemuende, the Bf 109 became an odds-on favorite. Demonstration of the Bf 109s ability to roll and recover at will, to maintain structural integrity under steep power dives from high altitudes, to turn inside and to outclimb the He 112, far outweighed the rumors and poor press that the new aircraft had been exposed to. Although not unanimous in its decision, the RLM recommended the selection of the Bf 109, and an order for 10 pre-production aircraft was placed with BFW.

Substantiation of this decision was to occur only weeks later when the Luftwaffe staged an aviation display at Rechlin for *Generalfeldmarschall* Goering and other high ranking officials of the RLM. The aerial display finished

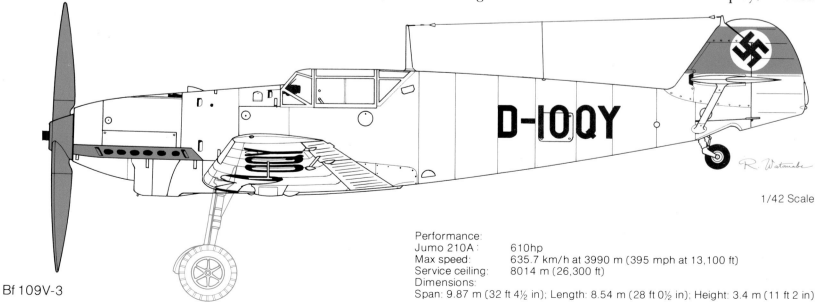

D-IOQY

R. Watanabe

1/42 Scale

Bf 109V-3

Performance:
Jumo 210A :   610hp
Max speed: 635.7 km/h at 3990 m (395 mph at 13,100 ft)
Service ceiling: 8014 m (26,300 ft)
Dimensions:
Span: 9.87 m (32 ft 4½ in); Length: 8.54 m (28 ft 0½ in); Height: 3.4 m (11 ft 2 in)

5

with a mock air battle in which a force of bombers were to be intercepted by a flight of four He 51s. After this interception, *Oberst* Ernst Udet (famous fighter ace of World War I) was to take off in the Bf 109A V3 and intercept the four He 51s. Udet took off and destroyed the four He 51s in simulated combat, and then, on his own initiative, attacked the bombers and was credited with destroying the entire formation in his new single-place fighter.

Bf 109B *series (pre-production)*

The Bf 109B-0 designation was allocated to pre-production aircraft to be utilized in optimizing the basic Bf 109 airframe, powerplant and armament. They were therefore assigned the standardized series of experimental, or 'V' codes that identified developmental aircraft. The initial Bf 109B, coded V4, closely resembled its Bf 109A predecessors in that it was fitted with the Junkers Jumo 210A. However, it incorporated an additional MG 17 machine-gun located between the cylinders of the engine and firing through the propeller hub. This added armament was installed in response to the Luftwaffe Operations Staff's final evaluation review of the prototype tests which noted that the original requirement for only a pair of the 7.9-mm weapons provided insufficient firepower.

The Bf 109 V4, flown for the first time in November, 1936, was followed during the next two months by the V5 and V6. These aircraft were fitted with the improved performance Jumo 210B powerplant and included other minor refinements consisting of the replacement of the gun cooling intake with a trio of flush cooling slots, a modified and strengthened forward windscreen, and a change in the wing support structure to allow for removal of the wing panel stiffeners added to the second prototype aircraft during undercarriage load testing.

Not only did these three aircraft successfully complete their pre-flight trials, but they were actually evaluated under combat conditions, when in December, 1936, and January, 1937, the three planes were shipped to *Jagdgruppe* 88 in Spain to assist the Nationalist cause in the Spanish Civil War. Germany had, in mid-1936, committed itself to support of the Nationalists and assigned *Jagdgruppe*

88, equipped with He 51s, to Seville. However, during the initial engagements between the He 51s of *Jagdgruppe* 88 and the Soviet-built Polikarpov I-15 fighters used by the Republican Forces, the German fighter had continuously been out performed. It was decided by the Luftwaffe Command to send the new experimental fighters into the conflict to evaluate their strong points and shortcomings.

As would be expected, the new aircraft suffered from the vast array of minor mechanical problems which normally plague the early development of new fighters. However, it did prove its superior performance in service operations and verified the decision of the *Luftwaffenfuehrungsstab* in selecting the Bf 109 over the He 112. The three fighters were subsequently returned to Augsburg to be reinstated into the planned development program.

Bf 109 V7 started its flight testing in March, 1937, and was fitted with a Jumo 210G powerplant with fuel injection and a two-stage supercharger that provided over 700 hp for take-off compared to the 610 hp rating of the earlier Jumo 210A. This aircraft was to serve as the prototype for the Bf 109B-2.

The V8, V9 and V10 aircraft were identified as prototypes for the Bf 109C. The V8 and V9 models were powered by the Jumo 210Ga powerplant, while the V10 aircraft, initially flown with the same powerplant, was re-engined with a high-performance DB 600Aa which delivered over 900 hp for take-off. The V8 incorporated a pair of wing-mounted MG 17 machine-guns just outside of the undercarriage strut which required a few simple modifications to the wing's leading edge, and firing trials proved so successful that the new four machine-gun armament was adopted as standard for the later Bf 109C.

The V9 was similar to the V8 except that it was fitted with a pair of 20-mm MG FF cannon in the wings in place of the 7.9-mm machine-guns. However, minor problems with the higher caliber weapon restricted its incorporation into the production of aircraft until the evolution of the E-version.

The V10 model, with its DB 600 powerplant, crashlanded during an attempt by Ernst Udet (who had become one of the Bf 109's most ardent supporters) to set speed records at the Zurich-Duebendorf International Flying Meeting in July, 1937, and was replaced by the V11

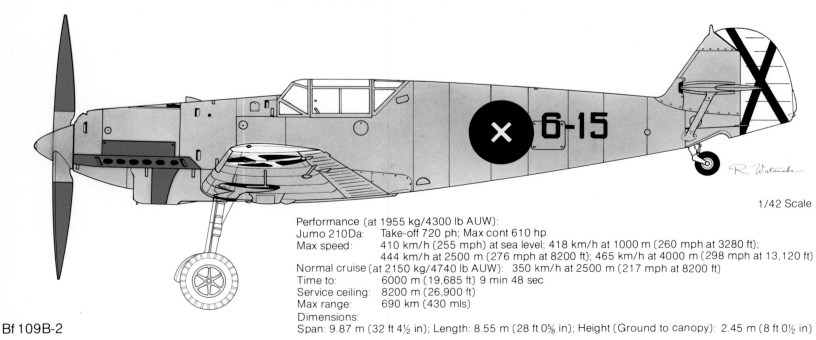

1/42 Scale

Bf 109B-2

Performance (at 1955 kg/4300 lb AUW):
Jumo 210Da: Take-off 720 ph; Max cont 610 hp
Max speed: 410 km/h (255 mph) at sea level; 418 km/h at 1000 m (260 mph at 3280 ft);
                  444 km/h at 2500 m (276 mph at 8200 ft); 465 km/h at 4000 m (298 mph at 13,120 ft)
Normal cruise (at 2150 kg/4740 lb AUW): 350 km/h at 2500 m (217 mph at 8200 ft)
Time to: 6000 m (19,685 ft) 9 min 48 sec
Service ceiling: 8200 m (26,900 ft)
Max range: 690 km (430 mls)
Dimensions:
Span: 9.87 m (32 ft 4½ in); Length: 8.55 m (28 ft 0⅝ in); Height (Ground to canopy): 2.45 m (8 ft 0½ in)

for powerplant testing of the new Daimler-Benz engine. The Bf 109 V12 and V13 (the last of the original pre-production prototypes) were also originally fitted with the DB 600A. The V13 aircraft was later re-engined with the new and more powerful DB 601 and was the aircraft which set the world airspeed record for land-based aircraft in November, 1937. Covering a 3-km (1.86-mile) straight course twice in both directions, the Bf 109 V13 was clocked at an average airspeed of 610.5 km/h (379.38 mph).

Bf 109B *series (production)*

With the impressive success of the early prototype Bf 109Bs, production of the variant was ordered, and the initial Bf 109B-1 rolled off the assembly lines in February, 1937. The B-1 was essentially based on the V4, V5, and V6 models of the pre-production run and were powered by the super-charged Jumo 210Da engine driving a Schwarz twin-blade fixed-pitch wooden propeller which provided 680 hp at take-off. The armament was limited to a pair of cowling-mounted MG 17 machine-guns, with the through-propeller hub machine-gun being omitted due to cooling problems uncovered during the testing of the V4, V5, and V6 aircraft.

Originally scheduled to go into service with *Jagdgeschwader* 132 "Richthofen," the initial B-1s were delivered to II *Gruppe* for combat training; however, the assignment of these aircraft to *Jagdgruppe* 88 in Spain was given top priority because of the proven advantages of the I-15 and I-16 over the Luftwaffe's He 51s. The pilots and aircraft of JG 132 therefore, were immediately transferred to *Jagdgruppe* 88 after training.

Only 30 of the B-1 models were produced before the *Luftwaffenfuehrungsstab* switched the Augsburg assembly line over to the Bf 109B-2, which differed from the B-1 only in the replacement of the wooden Schwarz airscrew with a variable-pitch VDM metal licence-built (Hamilton-Standard) propeller. By July, 1937, the Bf 109B-2s were being delivered to 1 *Staffel* of *Jagdgruppe* 88.

Because *Bayerische Flugzeugwerke* was producing the new fighter at maximum capacity, and still not meeting the Luftwaffe's need (although additional facilities were being constructed at Augsburg), a license agreement was signed with the Fieseler plant at Kassel for additional production. By December, aircraft from Fieseler began to supplement the deliveries from Augsburg.

Bf 190C *series*

The Bf 109C-1 was based on the V8, V9 and V10 prototype models and incorporated the improved Junkers Jumo 210Ga engine which developed 700 hp at take-off. (A few of the final batches of the Bf 109B-2 had been fitted with the Jumo 210Ga powerplant which was planned for initial incorporation into the Bf 109C.)

The C-1 also increased the basic Bf 109 armament through the addition of a pair of wing-mounted 7.9mm Rheinmetall MG 17 machine-guns and incorporated a revision of the powerplant exhaust exits and an increased radiator intake size which resulted in identifiable external differences from the B-1. In addition, the C-1 was fitted with an FuG 7 radio, providing direct communication between fighter-control ground forces and the plane, something that had not existed in the earlier models.

The Bf 109C-1s began leaving the assembly lines at Augsburg in March, 1938, and like its predecessors were immediately shipped to Spain to allow transition of the remaining He 51s and some of the initial Bf 109B-1s.

Three additional variants of the Bf 109C were produced at Augsburg, these being the C-2, C-3 and C-4 models. The Bf 109C-2 was an experimental development model and was identical to the C-1 except that it incorporated the engine-mounted MG 17 machine-gun that had been eliminated from earlier variants due to cooling problems. The cooling of the gun mechanism had been increased through a number of material changes and increases in insulation and ducting. The Bf 109C-3 was used as a test bed for the incorporation of using wing-mounted 20-mm MG FF cannons.

The Bf 109C-4, in turn, replaced the engine-mounted MG 17 with an MG FF cannon. The C-4s, however, were also utilized as developmental aircraft and were never delivered to operational units.

During the production of the C-version of the Bf 109, one other significant occurrence took place. That

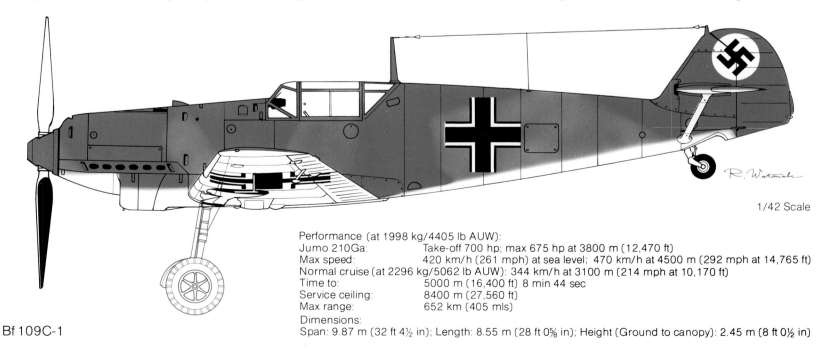

1/42 Scale

Bf 109C-1

Performance (at 1998 kg/4405 lb AUW):
Jumo 210Ga: Take-off 700 hp; max 675 hp at 3800 m (12,470 ft)
Max speed: 420 km/h (261 mph) at sea level; 470 km/h at 4500 m (292 mph at 14,765 ft)
Normal cruise (at 2296 kg/5062 lb AUW): 344 km/h at 3100 m (214 mph at 10,170 ft)
Time to: 5000 m (16,400 ft) 8 min 44 sec
Service ceiling: 8400 m (27,560 ft)
Max range: 652 km (405 mls)
Dimensions:
Span: 9.87 m (32 ft 4½ in); Length: 8.55 m (28 ft 0⅝ in); Height (Ground to canopy): 2.45 m (8 ft 0½ in)

was the change of name of the *Bayerische Flugzeugwerke* to *Messerschmitt A.G.* This change was essentially the result of not only the great success of the aircraft, but also because of the national hero status Messerschmitt had achieved during the previous two years with his innovative and successful new aircraft concepts. Wishing to capitalize on this growing fame, the German Air Ministry had suggested to the *Bayerische Flugzeugwerke* management (which included Messerschmitt) that it could provide the company with a more international image through the name change.

Bf 109D *series*

The Bf 109D version was produced only as an interim fighter (approximately 200 being built) filling the gap between the Jumo 210 powered Bf 109C and the planned DB 601 powered Bf 109E. The DB engines, both the basic 600 and the improved 601 models, provided increased performance to the Messerschmitt fighter. The availability of both, however, was limited during 1937-38. These limitations on availability were the influencing factors, not only on the decision to produce the D-variant, but also on the quantity built. Having been designed from the outset to accept the new Daimler-Benz 600 series powerplants, the incorporation of this engine into the Bf 109 was delayed until 1937 because the DB 600 was utilized in the He 111 bomber and the production of bombers had received the highest priorities during the mid-thirties. In addition, the service acceptance of the improved DB 601 engine was delayed due to difficulties with the new automatically-monitored supercharger system, which provided the engine with added power and eliminated cut-outs even under high G loadings.

    Realizing that the DB 600 would not be available in sufficient quantities for a large production run of the Bf 109D, and that the DB 601 would not be ready for some months, the German Air Ministry opted to produce the interim D-version with the limited supply of Jumo 210D and Jumo 210G powerplants, and to forestall the installation of the newer DB 601 until the Bf 109E series evolved.

    The Bf 109D program was initiated in mid-1937 with a pair of pre-production aircraft assigned the designation V14 and V15. However, these two planes were diverted to developmental efforts being started on the E-series aircraft, and the D-version was restricted to the utilization of the V11, V12 and V13 (Bf 109B-0 prototypes) for design and structural testing. The Bf 109D was to be the first model to feature the familiar lines that were to become the identification criteria for future variants. The aircraft would have been essentially identical to the earlier models from the cockpit aft, but the forward cowling would undergo a major change. The wide radiator intake would be replaced by a small, aerodynamically smooth, oil cooler intake and a pair of small glycol radiators would be added to the undersurface of each wing. A long supercharger air intake would also be added to the port side of the cowling just over the exhaust stubs. Structural strengthening was evident in the landing gear struts, undercarriage attach points and in the powerplant interface locations. However, all these modifications except for the structural changes, were delayed until the introduction of the E-version due to the reversion back to the Jumo powerplants.

    Armament for the Bf 109D consisted of the then-

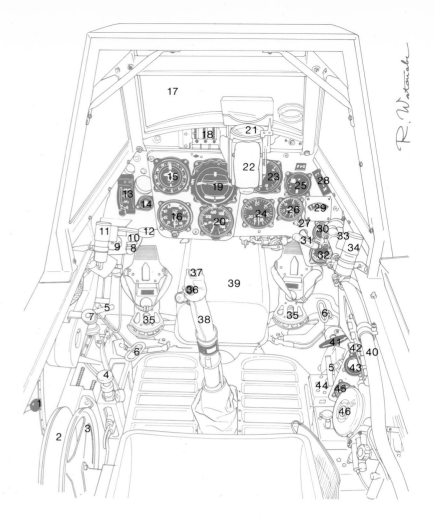

Bf 109G-6 Cockpit

1 Ventilation control lever
2 Undercarriage emergency lowering handwheel
3 Tailplane trim adjustment wheel
4 Fuel injection primer pump
5 Fuel cock lever
6 Radiator cut-off handle
7 Throttle
8 Undercarriage switch
9 Undercarriage position indicator
10 Undercarriage control switch
11 Instrument panel light
12 Canopy jettison lever
13 Ignition switch
14 Main light switch
15 Repeater compass
16 Altimeter
17 Laminated glass windscreen
18 Ammunition counters
19 Artificial horizon / turn and bank indicator
20 Airspeed indicator
21 Revi C/12D reflector gunsight. (Later series used Revi 16B)
22 Gunsight padding
23 Manifold pressure gauge
24 Tachometer
25 AFN2 homing indicator (for FuG16ZY only)
26 Propeller pitch position indicator
27 Fuel warning lamp
28 Tumbler switch
29 Combined coolant exit and oil intake temperature indicator
30 Fuel contents gauge
31 Undercarriage emergency release lever
32 Dual oil and fuel contents gauge
33 Auxiliary fuel contents indicator
34 Instrument panel light
35 Rudder pedal
36 Bomb release button
37 Firing trigger
38 Control column
39 20 mm MG151/20 cannon breech cover
40 Drop tank fuel pipe
41 Radiator shutter control lever
42 FuG16ZY radio control panel
43 Oxygen supply indicator
44 Oxygen pressure gauge
45 Radio control panel
46 Oxygen supply

1

2

3

4

5

6

7

8

9

10

11

12

13

14

15

16

17

18

19

20

21

22

23

24

25

26

27

28

29

30

(BUNDESARCHIV)

(BUNDESARCHIV)

R. Watanabe

Bf 109G-5/R2 flown by *Major* Hermann Graf, *Kommandeur* of JGr 50 (Jagdgruppe 50), 6 September, 1943.

The Bf 109G-5/R2 with the red tulip design on the nose and the Wfr.Gr.21 rocket mortars under both wings was flown by one of the best fighter pilots of the Luftwaffe, *Major* Hermann Graf, *Kommandeur* of *Jagdguppe* 50. He used it from summer 1943 until 22 March, 1944, when, as *Kommodore* of JG 11, he shot down two heavy US bombers but was himself badly wounded in a mid-air collision with a P-51 Mustang escort fighter.

Hermann Graf achieved his first victory on 3 August, 1941, flying as an *Oberfeldwebel* with JG 52. By 24 January, 1942, his score had risen to 42, and he was awarded the *Ritterkreuz* (Knights' Cross) and promoted to *Leutnant*. During the next four months Graf achieved another 62 victories on the Eastern Front increasing his score to 104, claiming his 100th on 14 May, 1942. Three days later he was awarded the Oak Leaves to the Knights' Cross as the 12th Luftwaffe pilot. By 4 September,

Graf's total had reached 150 victories, the second fighter pilot in the history to do so. Only twelve days later Graf's total had increased to 172 and he became the fifth Luftwaffe pilot to be awarded the Diamonds to the Oak Leaves and Swords of the Knights' Cross. However, on 2 October, 1942, after his 202nd victory, Graf was grounded by Propaganda Minister Goebbels who did not want to lose an exploitable national hero.

In early summer 1943 Graf was ordered to form and lead a special high-altitude unit, *Jagdgruppe* 50, remaining its *Kommandeur* until JGr 50 was disbanded in late autumn 1943. From November, 1943, to April, 1944, Graf was *Kommodore* of JG 11. After recuperation from his injuries Graf was appointed *Kommodore* of JG 52, and remained in this post until the capitulation with the rank of *Oberstleutnant*. By the end of the war Graf had flown 830 operational sorties and scored 212 confirmed victories.

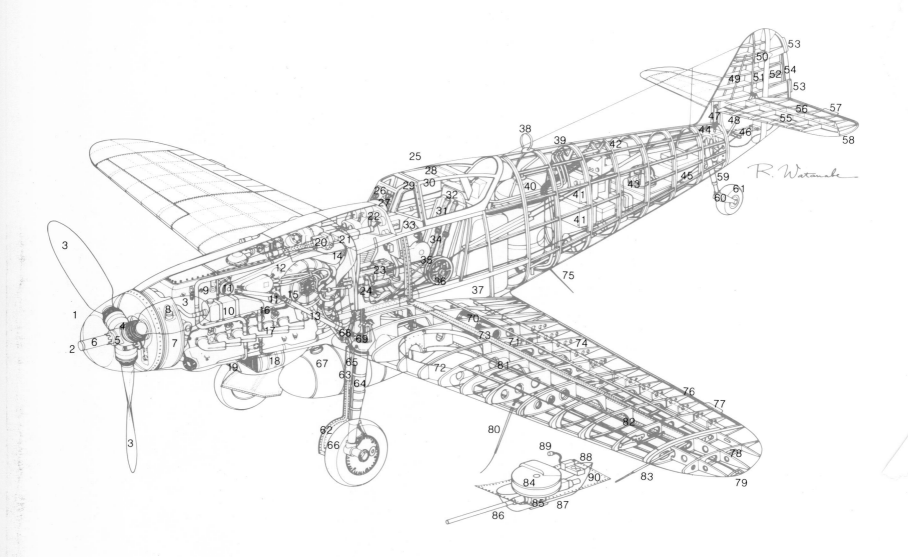

Bf 109 G-10 Cutaway

1 Spinner
2 Engine-mounted cannon muzzle
3 VDM 9-12159 electrically-operated constant-speed propeller
4 Propeller pitch-change mechanism
5 Propeller hub
6 Blast tube
7 Oil tank (50 ltr/11 Imp. gal capacity)
8 Oil filler cap
9 Daimler Benz DB 605DCM twelve-cylinder inverted-vee liquid-cooled engine
10 Coolant header tank
11 Anti-vibration rubber engine-mounting pads
12 Elektron forged engine bearer
13 Engine bearer support strut attachment
14 Engine bearer upper attachment
15 Supercharger assembly
16 Plug leads
17 Exhaust stubs
18 FO 987 oil cooler
19 Oil cooler intake
20 13-mm Rheinmetall Borsig MG 131 machine-gun breeches
21 13-mm machine-gun ammunition feed chute
22 Instrument panel
23 20-mm Mauser MG 151/20 cannon breech
24 Rudder pedals
25 'Galland'-type clear-vision hinged canopy
26 90-mm armourglass windscreen
27 Revi 16B reflector gunsight
28 Framed armourglass head/back panel

29 Armoured windshield frame
30 Canopy contoured frame
31 Pilot's seat
32 8-mm back armour
33 Throttle lever
34 Seat harness
35 Tail trim handwheel (in board)
36 Undercarriage emergency retraction handwheel (out board)
37 Underfloor contoured fuel tank (400 ltr/88 Imp. gal, 96 octane C3)
38 D/F loop antenna
39 Main fuel filler cap
40 MW 50 (methanol/water) tank (114 ltr/25 Imp. gal capacity)
41 Wireless equipment packs FuG16ZY (VHF 38.5 – 42.3MHz communications and FuG 25a IFF)
42 Methanol tank
43 Master compass
44 Tail trimming cables
45 Rudder cables
46 Rudder actuating linkage
47 Elevator control quadrant
48 Elevator connecting rod
49 All-wooden tailfin construction
50 Rudder upper hinge bracket
51 Rudder post
52 Fabric-covered wooden rudder structure
53 Fixed rudder trim tub
54 Geared rudder tub
55 Tailplane structure
56 Port elevator
57 Fixed elevator trim tub

58 Elevator balance
59 Castoring non-retractable tailwheel leg
60 Wheel housing
61 Tailwheel tire: 350×135 mm (13.8×5.3 in)
62 Mainwheel fairing
63 Mainwheel leg fairing
64 Mainwheel oleo leg
65 Brake lines
66 Port mainwheel
67 Auxilliary fuel tank (Rüstsatz R3), 300 ltr (66 Imp. gal)
68 Undercarriage retraction jak mechanism
69 Undercarriage pivot/bevel
70 Ducted coolant radiator
71 Flap actuating linkage
72 Port mainwheel well
73 Wing spar
74 Slotted flap structure
75 FuG 25a antenna
76 Metal-framed Frise-type aileron
77 Fixed trim tub
78 Wingtip construction
79 Port navigation light
80 FuG16ZY Morane antenna
81 Slot equalizer rod
82 Wing ribs
83 Pitot tube
84 Ammunition magazine drum
85 20-mm Mausar MG151/20 cannon
86 Cannon barrel
87 Gondola fairing
88 Electrical junction box
89 14-point plug connection
90 Underwing panel

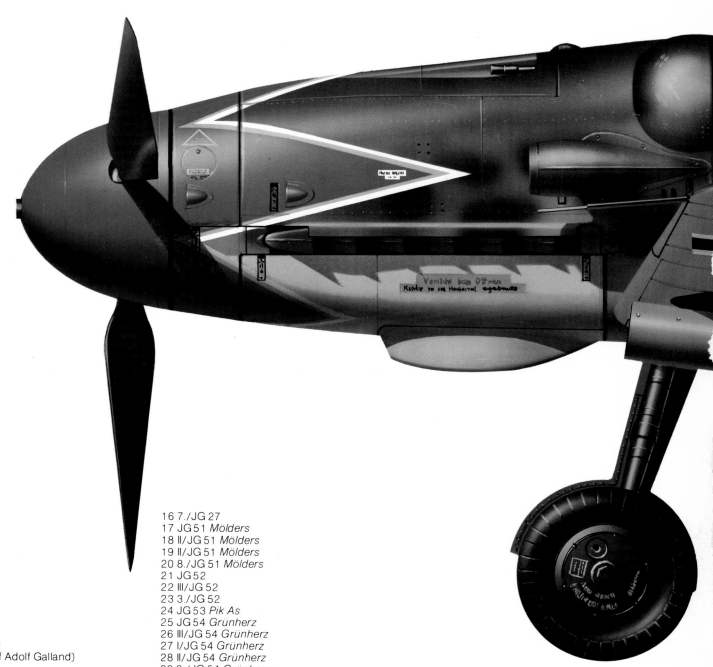

Emblems

1 JG 1
2 JG 2 *Richthofen*
3 III./JG 2 *Richthofen*
4 7./JG 2 *Richthofen*
5 JG 3 *Udet*
6 II./JG 3 *Udet*
7 III./JG 11
8 JG 26 *Schlageter*
9 Stab III./JG 26 *Schlageter*
10 5./JG 26 *Schlageter*
11 9./JG 26 *Schlageter*
12 Erg. Staffel/JG 26 *Schlageter*
13 Galland (Personal emblem of Adolf Galland)
14 I/JG 27
15 III./JG 27 (previously I/JG 1)

16 7./JG 27
17 JG 51 *Mölders*
18 II./JG 51 *Mölders*
19 II./JG 51 *Mölders*
20 8./JG 51 *Mölders*
21 JG 52
22 III./JG 52
23 3./JG 52
24 JG 53 *Pik As*
25 JG 54 *Grünherz*
26 III./JG 54 *Grünherz*
27 I/JG 54 *Grünherz*
28 II./JG 54 *Grünherz*
29 9./JG 54 *Grünherz*
30 I/JG 77 (previously I/LG 2)

◀ **Left**
Bf 109F-4, flown by *Hauptmann* Reinhard Seiler, *Kommandeur*, III./JG 54, on the Eastern Front at the end of 1941. His final rank was *Major* and he scored 109 victories in total including 16 night victories over Russia.

◀ **Right**
Oberleutnant Hans-Ekkehard Bob, *Staffelkapitän*, 9./JG 54 and his Bf 109F-2 on the Eastern Front in the winter of 1941–42. His final rank was *Major* and he scored 59 victories in total including 21 victories on the Western Front.

1   2

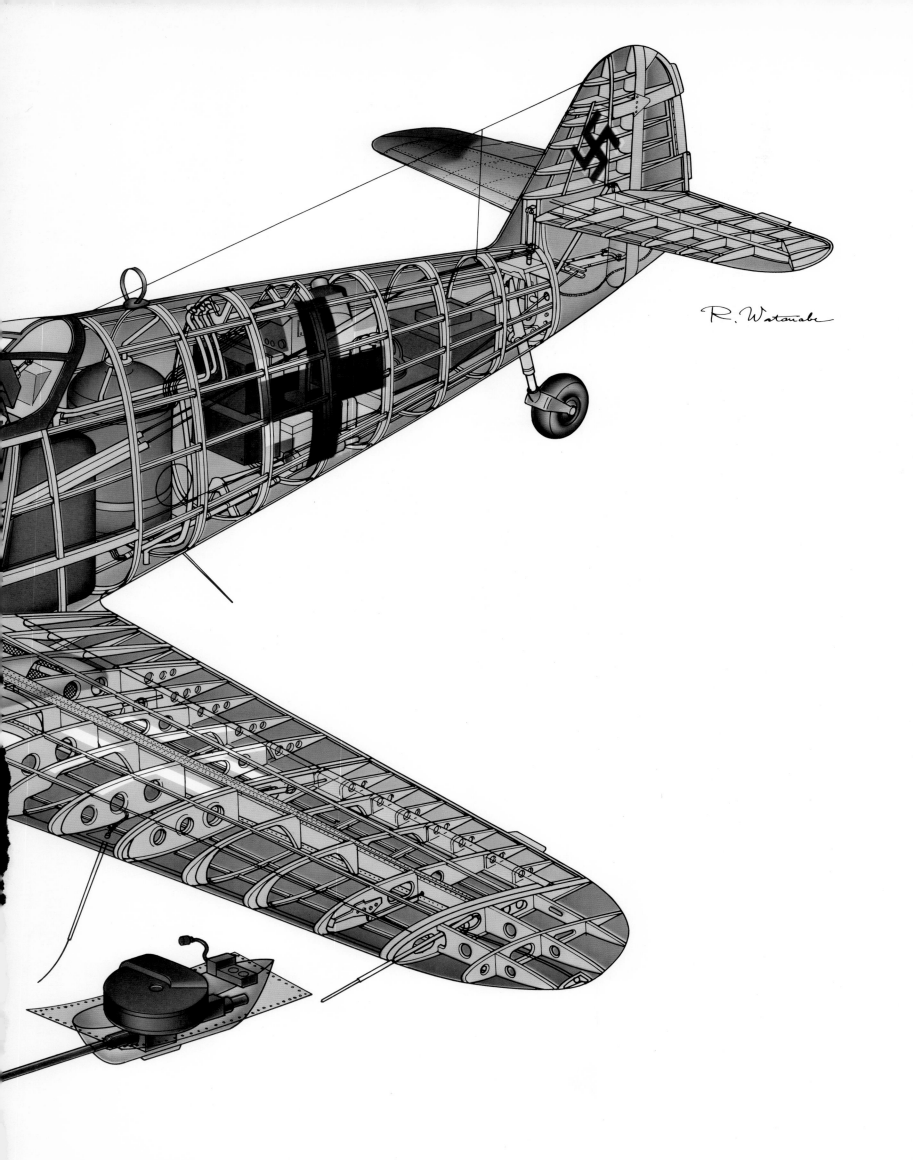

R. Watanabe

Bf 109D, I/ZG 2, summer, 1939.

(BUNDESARCHIV)

standardized pair of cowl-mounted MG 17 machine-guns and a single 20-mm MG FF cannon between the cylinders of the inverted-Vee Jumo powerplant. The latter weapon was later removed from some of the aircraft, as operational use still resulted in numerous occurrences of jamming, and flight characteristics were adversely influenced when the cannon was fired.

In an effort to increase armament and overcome the still unresolved engine-mounted weapon problems, the Bf 109D-2 was ordered. The D-2 was identical to the D-1 except that the center-mounted weapon was omitted and the aircraft was fitted with a pair of wing-mounted MG 17 machine-guns. In addition, a small number of Bf 109D-3s were produced that differed from the D-2 only in that they incorporated a pair of 20-mm MG FF cannon in the wings in place of the MG 17 machine-guns.

Bf 109E *series*

The first large scale production version of the Bf 109 series was the Bf 109E. Powered by the DB 601A-1 engine, which had been fitted to the first pair of pre-production Bf 109D-0

aircraft (V14 and V15), ten pre-production Bf 109E-0s were ordered for service evaluation; basically for acceptance testing of the new powerplant. The testing of the DB 601 was necessitated by the RLM's decision to cancel further production of the DB 600 in early 1938 based on promises from Daimler-Benz that production quantities of the DB 601 would be available for the E-series by mid-1938. Problems with the early DB 601s, however, had delayed its service acceptance, and thus, production of the Bf 109E.

Assigning the first three pre-production codes (Bf 109E-01, -02, and -03) to the Bf 109 V13, V14, and V15, the remaining seven pre-production aircraft received designations of V16 through V22. These were utilized to test various armament and engine modifications.

Production deliveries of the Bf 109E-1 began early in 1939 with several of the initial aircraft being assigned to Spain with the Condor Legion, which began receiving the Bf 109E during February and March. Although these aircraft arrived too late to influence the outcome of the Spanish Civil War, a few scattered encounters between the new variant and the aircraft of the Republican Forces did take place, with the Bf 109E proving its vast superiority in almost every category.

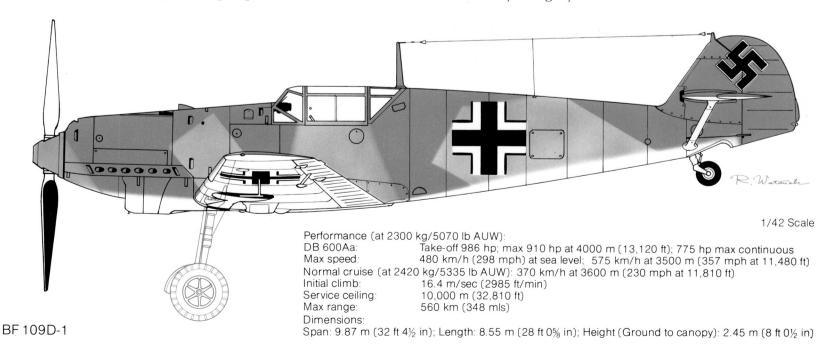

1/42 Scale

BF 109D-1

Performance (at 2300 kg/5070 lb AUW):
DB 600Aa: Take-off 986 hp; max 910 hp at 4000 m (13,120 ft); 775 hp max continuous
Max speed: 480 km/h (298 mph) at sea level; 575 km/h at 3500 m (357 mph at 11,480 ft)
Normal cruise (at 2420 kg/5335 lb AUW): 370 km/h at 3600 m (230 mph at 11,810 ft)
Initial climb: 16.4 m/sec (2985 ft/min)
Service ceiling: 10,000 m (32,810 ft)
Max range: 560 km (348 mls)
Dimensions:
Span: 9.87 m (32 ft 4½ in); Length: 8.55 m (28 ft 0⅝ in); Height (Ground to canopy): 2.45 m (8 ft 0½ in)

Bf 109E-4/Trop, I/JG 27, North Africa.   (BUNDESARCHIV)   Bf 109E-4/Trop, I/JG 27, North Africa.   (BUNDESARCHIV)

Armament of the early Bf 109E-1 included the standardized pair of cowl-mounted 7.9-mm MG 17 machine-guns and a pair of the same weapons installed in the wings. However, based on the successful results of both testing with the V14, and the favoring of heavier armament by the RLM, later batches of the E-1 were produced with a pair of 20-mm MG FF cannon in place of the wing-mounted machine-guns. Due to the increased size of the cannons, a specially designed cover with a bulged shape was fitted to the lower wing to provide space for the larger weapon and its ammunition drum. In addition, a selector switch for control of both, or one, of the wing weapons was installed in the cockpit allowing the pilot a choice of firepower.

By the end of the hostilities in Spain in late March, 1939, only twenty of the planned 40 Bf 109E-1s had been delivered to *Jagdgruppe* 88. Although the Luftwaffe units in Germany were also re-equipping with the Bf 109E at this time, the twenty aircraft were transferred to the Spanish National Forces, along with the remaining Bf 109Bs and Bf 109Cs.

The next variant of the Bf 109E to reach production was the E-3, incorporating the improved DB 601Aa which delivered nearly 1,200 hp at take-off and had provision for the installation of an MG FF cannon between the powerplant's cylinders. Problems of jamming, overheating and vibration, however, still plagued this modification, and most of the installations were either removed in the field, or seldom used. The Bf 109E-3 also incorporated other modifications, including a revised canopy design with heavier frame, and the addition of armor plate behind the pilot's head and under the seat.

The Bf 109E-3 supplanted the Bf 109E-1 on the assembly lines in late 1939 and by the end of the year they had started arriving for operational service with frontline Luftwaffe units.

Because of the apparent failure of the nose-mounted MG FF cannon, and its subsequent removal after installation, it was decided to produce the Bf 109E-3 without the center-firing weapon. The result was the designation change to Bf 109E-4, with production deliveries beginning during the summer of 1940.

It was also during this time that thoughts of employing the Bf 109 as a *Jagdbomber* (fighter-bomber) were being considered, based on the needs developed during fighting against the French. The concept was to attach a single bomb under the center fuselage and provide the pilot with an electrical release switch. To test the theory, an evaluation unit, *Erprobungsgruppe* 210, was formed and a number of Bf 109E-1s and Bf 110Cs were assigned as test aircraft.

With only very minimal training in dive-bombing techniques, the unit began their operational testing against British shipping in the English Channel. The results of the limited endeavor proved so successful that all Luftwaffe *Jagdgeschwader* were ordered to form one *Staffel* for *Jabo* operations. Normally consisting of nine *Staffeln*, this usually meant the addition of a tenth unit. To equip these new units, Bf 109E-1s, which were being replaced by the later model Bf 109E-3s and E-4s, were retrofitted with an ETC 50 rack for the carrying of a 50 kg (110-lb.) SC 50 bomb and assigned the designation Bf 109-E-1/B. In addition, several Bf 109E-4s still on the assembly lines were converted to Bf 109E-4/Bs through the incorporation of a central ETC 250 rack which was capable of handling a single 250 kg (550-lb.) bomb or four SC 50 bombs.

Continuing to strive for ever increasing performance, Daimler-Benz developed the DB 601N powerplant which not only delivered 1,200 hp at take-off, but also offered an emergency output of 1,250 hp for a duration of 1 minute at altitudes in the 4500 m (15,000 ft) range. The engine made use of flattened piston heads instead of the normal concave shape and increased the compression ratio by 15%. Due to this higher compression ratio the powerplant also required the use of higher octane fuel, necessitating a change from 87 to 96 octane. This powerplant was installed into the Bf 109E-4 series in mid-1940 and the aircraft were given the designation of Bf 109E-4/N.

The Bf 109E-5 was identical to the standard Bf 109E-4 except that it included the installation of a Rb 21/18 camera in the aft fuselage and deleted the wing-mounted MG FF cannon. Produced side-by-side with the E-4, the E-5 was assigned the task of fighter-reconnaissance. With the elimination of the wing armament and ammunition the aircraft's overall weight was reduced to give it increased airspeed for escape from Allied fighter-interceptors. A further refinement of the basic fighter-reconnaissance concept was reflected in the Bf 109E-6, which was identical to the E-5 model, except that it incorporated the higher performance DB 601N which had first been installed on the Bf 109E-4/N.

The next Bf 109E variant to appear was the E-7 which was identical to the Bf 109E-4/N except that it included a factory-installed ventrally-mounted ETC 250 rack capable of interfacing with an expendable auxiliary fuel tank (for extended range operation), or with an SC 250 bomb for use as a long-range fighter-bomber. This variant was further modified during 1941 to include the Bf 109E-7/U2, an early *Umruest-Bausatz* (factory conversion kit) which provided added armor plate protection for the underwing radiators, lower powerplant area and fuel tanks, and the Bf 109E-7/Z which incorporated a GM 1 injectant boost system to the engine. The injectant system tank, located behind the cockpit, contained nitrous oxide in liquid form which was fed to the powerplant by compressed air and injected into the supercharger where it provided added oxygen. This was, of course, advantageous at higher altitudes where the oxygen level is reduced, and the engine, dependent on oxygen for combustion, starts losing power. The injectant system, in effect, acted as an artificial altitude compensator.

The final two basic variants of the E-series were the Bf 109E-8 and the Bf 109E-9, which made their initial appearance in late 1940. The E-8 was almost identical to the basic E-1 variant, in that it was armed with a pair of fuselage-mounted MG 17 machine-guns and a similar pair of wing-mounted weapons. Designated as an extended-range fighter, the E-8 was fitted with the underfuselage rack to carry an auxiliary drop tank. The E-9 model was a combination of several of the earlier innovations and modifications made on the E-series and was assigned the role of long-range photo-reconnaissance. The aircraft, powered by the DB 601N engine, was fitted with the auxiliary fuel tank rack, and incorporated an Rb 50/30 camera aft of the cockpit. Armament consisted of the MG 17 fuselage machine-guns, and a pair of wing-mounted MG FF cannon.

Many other supplemental modifications were made to the basic Bf 109 E-series during its production career — late 1939 through early 1942. These included tropicalized versions of the Bf 109E-4, -5 and -7. The tropicalized modifications, resulting from the dusty environment of the North African area, included the installation of a filter over and in front of the supercharger air intake on the port side of the engine cowling and the packaging of a desert survival kit (including a lightweight carbine, food and water supply, signal equipment, etc.) inside the aircraft. The tropicalized versions of the Bf 109 were given the designation Trop. This term appeared after the basic model designation, as in Bf 109-5/Trop.

Several one-of-a-kind experimental projects were also conducted with the Bf 109E series including the use of skis and the incorporation of overwing or underwing fuel tanks. The idea behind the use of skis was to provide for operations from snow covered landing areas and, even possibly, deep sand. A Bf 109E-8 was fitted with a pair of faired skis in place of wheels (in actuality, the skis appeared to be more like hollow pontoons) and was flight tested both with the skis alone and using a jettisonable wheeled dolly for assist in take-offs. By the time the tests had been completed, experience by the Luftwaffe in actual winter environments had resulted in minimal difficulties, and as the skied version of the Bf 109E suffered in performance due to the increased drag of the skis and fairings, the project was dropped.

The use of jettisonable over and under wing fuel tanks to improve the range of the fighter was tested on a modified Bf109E-4 in 1942. It was shown that the installation of these contoured tanks did not appreciably reduce overall airspeed, although they did, to a minor degree, decrease the aircraft's turning rate and overall handling characteristics. Because the need for this type of range was not critical (due in part to the installation of ventraly mounted drop tanks), the basic concept was cancelled. However, the possibility of utilizing the over-wing containers to carry personnel and equipment on behind-the-lines espionage missions added new life to the program. In the summer of 1943, a Bf 109E-4 had been modified with re-contoured over-wing containers capable of carrying a man, his parachute and necessary survival equipment, and was test-flown at Stuttgart-Ruit. Tests showed only a minimal loss in airspeed. By this time, however, interest in the project had subsided and no evidence exists that this concept was ever put to actual practice.

Bf 109F *series*

In early 1940, the Augsburg plant began a design improvement program with the intent of incorporating not only structural and aerodynamic modifications to the basic Bf 109 airframe, but also the installation of the higher per-

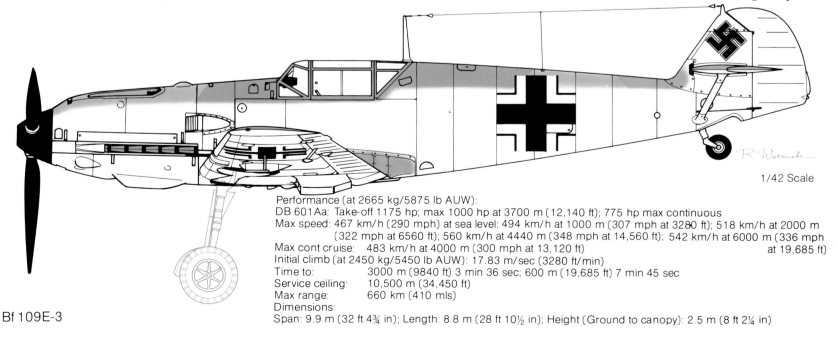

1/42 Scale

Performance (at 2665 kg/5875 lb AUW):
DB 601Aa: Take-off 1175 hp; max 1000 hp at 3700 m (12,140 ft); 775 hp max continuous
Max speed: 467 km/h (290 mph) at sea level; 494 km/h at 1000 m (307 mph at 3280 ft); 518 km/h at 2000 m (322 mph at 6560 ft); 560 km/h at 4440 m (348 mph at 14,560 ft); 542 km/h at 6000 m (336 mph at 19,685 ft)
Max cont cruise: 483 km/h at 4000 m (300 mph at 13,120 ft)
Initial climb (at 2450 kg/5450 lb AUW): 17.83 m/sec (3280 ft/min)
Time to: 3000 m (9840 ft) 3 min 36 sec; 600 m (19,685 ft) 7 min 45 sec
Service ceiling: 10,500 m (34,450 ft)
Max range: 660 km (410 mls)
Dimensions:

Bf 109E-3

Span: 9.9 m (32 ft 4¾ in); Length: 8.8 m (28 ft 10½ in); Height (Ground to canopy): 2.5 m (8 ft 2¼ in)

Daimler Benz DB 601A engine

Year:	1937
Type:	12-cylinder inverted 60 degrees Vee supercharged liquid-cooled engine
Bore:	150 mm
Stroke:	160 mm
Total swept capacity:	33.9 lit (2069 in³)
Compression ratio:	6.9 : 1
Fuel:	92 octane
Maximum RPM:	2400 rpm
Reduction gearing:	1 : 1.55
Dry weight:	610 kg (1,344.7 lb)
Length:	1,352 mm (4 ft 5¼ in)
Width:	705 mm (2 ft 3¾ in)
Height:	1,027 mm (3 ft 4½ in)

Take-off power:	1,100 hp. max 1 min
Rated power at height:	1,020 hp at 4,500 m (14,800 ft), max 5 mins
Maximum continuous power:	960 hp at 5,000 m (16,400 ft), max 30 mins
Maximum cruise power:	890 hp at 5,700 m (18,700 ft)
Maximum economical cruise power:	800 hp at 5,500 (18,000 ft)

1. Top cover of crankcase
2. Crankcase
3. Oil distributing joint
4. Reduction gear
5. Propeller shaft flange
6. Coolant injection pipe
7. Cylinder block
8. Spark plug
9. Air hose
10. Pilot pipe for coolant
11. Exhaust port
12. Bleeder
13. Balanced crankshaft
14. Connecting rod
15. Piston and rings
16. Valve
17. Valve spring
18. Overhead camshaft
19. Suction pipe (from oil feedback pump)
20. Ignition magnet
21. Hook-up bracket
22. Engine mount connecting joint
23. Air filter
24. Supercharger casing
25. Oil feedback pump
26. Valve gear cover

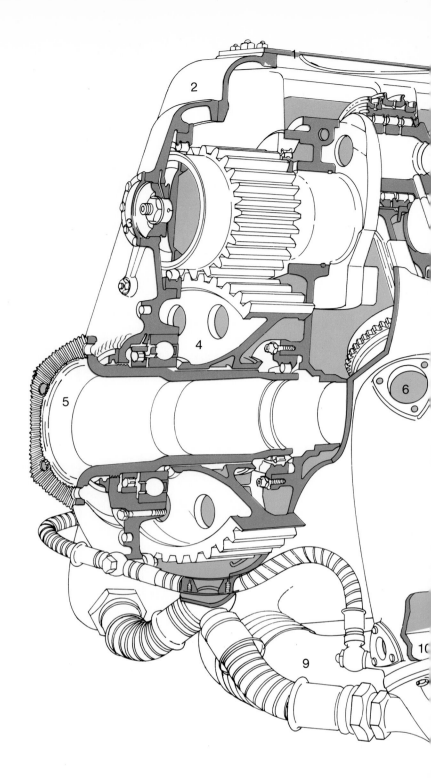

BF 109F-2/JG 54, Eastern Front. An armourer prepares to load the nose-mounted 20 mm MG151/20 cannon.

forming powerplants that were then under development at Daimler-Benz. The result of this program was the Bf 109F.

The airframe changes were numerous and resulted in an external configuration that was to remain essentially unchanged through the remainder of the Bf 109 variants. The wing, which had remained the same since the initial prototypes of the basic Bf 109, maintained the primary contours and spar structure, but incorporated a pair of significant modifications to reduce drag and improve lifting characteristics. First, the underwing radiators, which were a large contributor to the aircraft's drag, were decreased in height and recessed deeper into the wing through the use of a unique system of flaps and ducts which reduced the turbulence normally associated with the radiator protrusion into the airstream. The installation of this system also resulted in a change in the length and span of both the leading and trailing edge control flaps and the

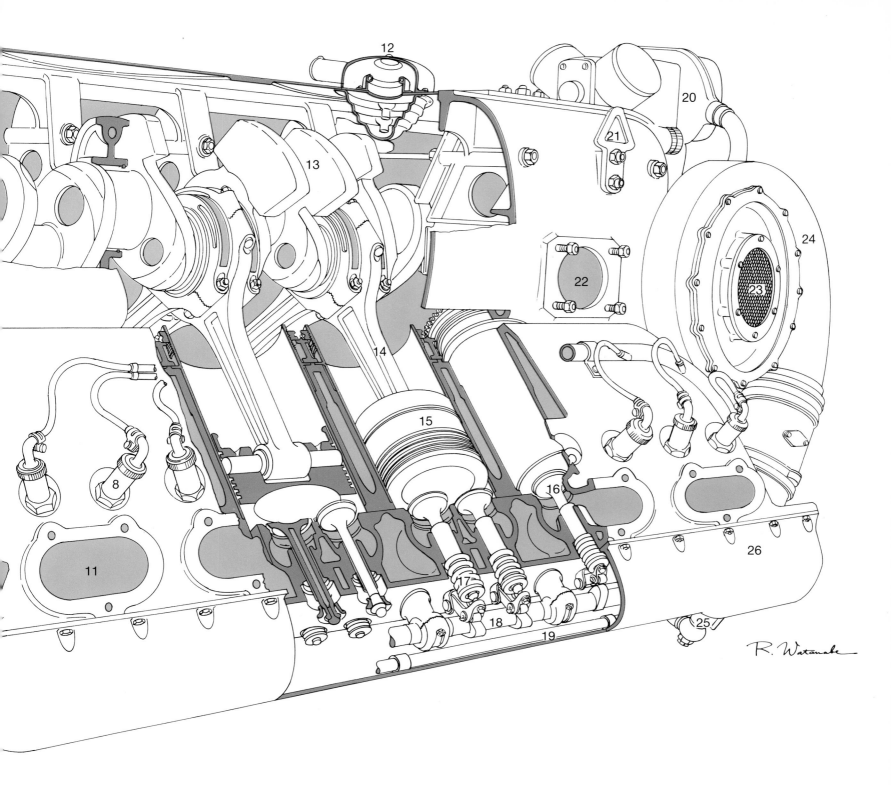

elimination of interconnecting linkage between the flaps and ailerons fitted previously.

A deeper, more streamlined cowling was also designed which tapered directly from the forward windscreen to the propeller hub and the air intake for the supercharger was moved farther into the airstream to increase the ram-effect of the scooped in air. The propeller hub, or spinner, was enlarged and lengthened to fit the new symmetrical cowling and contoured to reduce turbulent drag factors. In addition, the overall airscrew diameter was reduced by 10 cm (4 in) through the use of wider blades.

Major modifications also were incorporated into the tail assembly section where the rudder area was slightly reduced and the tail-plane bracing struts, which had become an identifying feature of earlier Bf 109s, were removed. With the removal of the struts, the new cantilevered tail-plane was moved slightly forward and below the

DB 601N engine   (BUNDESARCHIV)

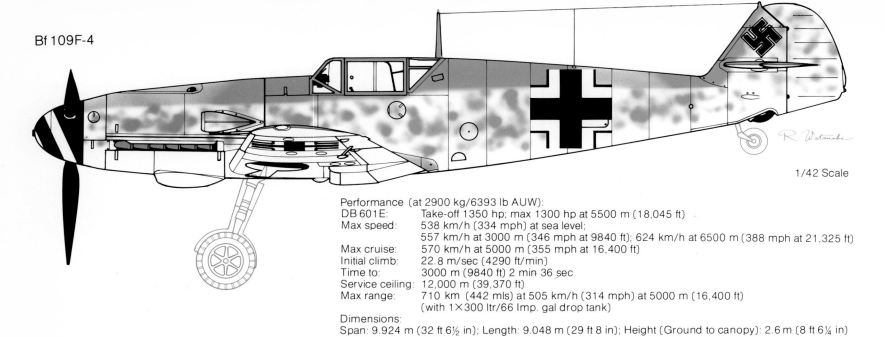

Bf 109F-4

1/42 Scale

Performance (at 2900 kg/6393 lb AUW):
DB 601E: Take-off 1350 hp; max 1300 hp at 5500 m (18,045 ft)
Max speed: 538 km/h (334 mph) at sea level;
             557 km/h at 3000 m (346 mph at 9840 ft); 624 km/h at 6500 m (388 mph at 21,325 ft)
Max cruise: 570 km/h at 5000 m (355 mph at 16,400 ft)
Initial climb: 22.8 m/sec (4290 ft/min)
Time to: 3000 m (9840 ft) 2 min 36 sec
Service ceiling: 12,000 m (39,370 ft)
Max range: 710 km (442 mls) at 505 km/h (314 mph) at 5000 m (16,400 ft)
             (with 1×300 ltr/66 Imp. gal drop tank)
Dimensions:
Span: 9.924 m (32 ft 6½ in); Length: 9.048 m (29 ft 8 in); Height (Ground to canopy): 2.6 m (8 ft 6¼ in)

original positioning and the chord thickness increased for structural rigidity.

Planned for installation of the DB 601E engine, which provided 1,350 hp for take-off, the four Bf 109F prototypes and ten pre-production aircraft were initiated in May, 1940. However, service testing and acceptance of the DB 601E had not yet been completed and, as a consequence, powerplant substitutions had to be made.

The first prototype, Bf 109 V21 utilized the DB 601Aa which had powered the later E-series while the last three prototypes all had early development DB 601E's installed. The Bf 109 V22 was to be utilized primarily for testing of the powerplant while the V23 and V24 aircraft were scheduled to be used for minor modifications to the new design in the area of structural and flight handling characteristics. The most significant change from the initial Bf 109F configuration was incorporated into V23, when el-

Oberleuntnant Viktor Bauer of JG 3 *Udet* achieved a total of 109 victories.

(BUNDESARCHIV)

liptically shaped detachable wingtips were added to increase the wing surface area (reducing wing loading) and to restore overall wingspan dimensions that had been reduced with the incorporation of the improved underwing radiator system. Armament for the Bf 109F was standardized with the retention of the cowling-mounted 7.9-mm MG 17 machine-guns and the addition of a 20-mm MG 151 cannon firing through the hollow propeller shaft. The reduction in armament from the Bf 109E, which had either a pair of MG 17 machine-guns or MG FF cannon mounted in the wings, was the result of several operational pilots' reports which maintained that the concentrated firepower of the center located weapons was more effective than the converging fire of the wing mounted weapons and that, in addition, the elimination of the wing armament added to the aircraft's handling characteristics.

Due to the continued delay in delivery of the planned DB 601E, the ten pre-production Bf 109F-0s, which began rolling off the assembly lines in October 1940, were powered by the DB 601N engine with its flattened piston heads. The F-0s also were fitted with the older MG FF cannon in the nose as deliveries of the proposed electronically armed MG 151/15 and MG 151/20 (15-mm and 20-mm) were delayed.

Deliveries of the initial Bf 109F-1 variant, very similar to its predecessor, the Bf 109F-0, began in November. The only real discernible difference in appearance was in the installation of the new extended supercharger air intake. This replaced the rectangular flush-mounted air intake from the E-series that had been used on the early pre-production aircraft until tests of the optimum contour and inlet size were completed on the improved design.

Within a few weeks of the initial deliveries of the Bf 109F-1s to Luftwaffe service evaluation units a number of them were lost, with the only clue as to the cause being a few pilot's messages reporting violent vibrations just prior to complete loss of control and crash. The Bf 109Fs were grounded and the cause of the vibration problem was investigated, with concentration in the powerplant attach interfaces and structural supports. Finding no irregularities, the investigation centered on the tail assembly, and it was discovered that the removal of the bracing struts had resulted in a high frequency vibration being set up in the fuselage at certain engine rpm levels. The aircraft were

retrofitted with reinforcing plates in the tail-plane to fuse-lage attachment area and production was resumed.

In February and March, 1941, deliveries of the Bf 109F-1 gave way to the production of the Bf 109F-2 which varied from the F-1 only in that it replaced the nose-mounted MG FF cannon with the long awaited MG 151. The F-2 variant also was modified through the incorporation of a fuselage-mounted ETC 250 bomb rack or the addition of the GM 1 nitrous oxide power boost system on a number of aircraft. As the Luftwaffe had not standardized either the *Umruest-Bausatze* (factory installed modifications which were intended to increase performance or to utilize non-strategic materials) or the *Ruestsaetze* (bolt-on modifications that were added to the Bf 109 airframe for specific mission capabilities such as extended range and increased arma-ment, and which could be incorporated either at the assem-bly line or in the field), the above noted modifications to the F-2 variant resulted in the designations of Bf 109F-2/Z (addi-tion of GM 1 boost system) and the Bf 109F-2/B (addition of the ETC 250 ventral bomb rack) fighter-bomber. One further designation was allocated to the F-2 series, the Bf 109F-2/Trop, which was the tropicalized version. Like the previous Bf 109E-4/Trop, this sub-type was fitted with a dust filter over the supercharger air intake for use in the North African theater of operations.

The Bf 109F-3 and Bf 109F-4, which were produced simultaneously, replaced the F-2 variant on the assembly lines in early 1942 and differed from the F-2 in that they incorporated the long awaited DB 601E as the basic pow-erplant. The powerplant change was the only difference between the F-2 and F-3; however, the F-4 incorporated a number of additional modifications that were not exter-nally discernible. These included an increase in the calibre of the MG 151 from 15-mm to 20-mm, the use of new self sealing fuel tanks, and an increase in the armor protection for the pilot. This protection included a thick steel plate behind the pilot's neck and upper back, and a similar plate mounted over his head under the bullet-resistant canopy glass. Both the F-3 and F-4 utilized the FuG 7a radio transmitter/receiver and Revi C/12D reflector gunsight that were standard on the earlier F-series.

A number of Bf 109F-4s were also modified like the F-2 variant with the incorporation of the GM 1 nitrous oxide boost system (Bf 109F-4/Z). In addition, two further

sub-type conversions were produced under the Bf 109F-4 designation. The first of these was the Bf 109F-4/R6 which was fitted with an extra pair of 20-mm MG 151 cannon in underwing gondolas. The increase in firepower was made at the request of General Adolf Galland and other top Luftwaffe fighter aces. The additional armament of the F-4/R6 was well received. The increased weight and added drag had a detrimental effect on the aircraft's handling qualities, however, reducing its capability as a "dogfighter," and the aircraft were used strictly as bomber-interceptors.

The second conversion was similar to that of the earlier fighter-bomber modifications to the Bf 109E-4/B and included the attachment of the ventrally-mounted ETC 250 bomb rack capable of carrying a 250 kg (550 lb) bomb, a 300 l (66 Imp gal) jettisonable fuel tank, or with an ER 4 adapter, four 50 kg (110 lb) SC 50 bombs.

The final two variants of the Bf 109F series were reconnaissance derivatives of the Bf 109F-4. The Bf 109F-5 eliminated the nose mounted cannon (for reduced weight and, thus, higher speed) and had a Rb 50/30 camera mounted in the aft fuselage. The Bf 109F-6 eliminated all armament and was fitted with a special camera bay in the underside of the fuselage just aft of the cockpit which was capable of utilizing the Rb 20/30, Rb 50/30 or RB 75/30 cameras. Both the F-5 and F-6 were fitted with a fuselage rack (R3 modification) for the 300 l (66 Imp gal) auxiliary fuel tank.

Bf 109G *series*

During late 1941 and early 1942, the RLM became increas-ingly concerned with higher aircraft speeds and was willing to accept higher wing and power loading risks. The neces-sity for a pressurized canopy was also among the require-ments for higher altitude capability. The Bf 109G was to be their answer.

The G-version was planned to utilize the im-proved performance DB 605A powerplant with a take-off output of 1,450 hp and 1,250 hp at 20,000 feet. The only difference in the DB 605A and the then-popular DB 601E was that the new powerplant had a redesigned block which allowed oversized cylinders while maintaining the same centers. The increased volume raised the compression ratio

Hauptmann Gerhard Barkhorn, *Gruppenkommandeur*, II/JG 52 is congratulated on his 250th victory in his Bf109G-6/Trop *Christl.* 13 February, 1944. (BUNDESARCHIV)

while the basic dimensions of the overall engine remained the same. The installation of the DB 605A into the Bf 109G airframe, however, resulted in numerous structural changes as the new powerplant was not only more powerful (in torque), but was also heavier. As a consequence the weight spiral of the overall Bf 109 design continued upward, reducing handling and maneuvering characteristics.

To provide the necessary cockpit pressurization, Messerschmitt simply sealed the bulkheads, floorplate and sidewalls, incorporated a plate behind the pilot which seated with the fuselage wall on closure, and added seals to the hinged and open rails at the canopy to fuselage interfaces.

Construction of twelve pre-production Bf 109G-0s was started during the late summer of 1941, but the un-availability of the proposed DB 605A powerplant forced Messerschmitt to again substitute, this time with the DB 601E. The pre-production block was completed by October, 1941, and immediately, Messerschmitt set about initiation of the first production aircraft under the designation Bf 109G-1. The G-1, deliveries of which began in March, 1942, was fitted with a pressurized cockpit, incorporated the radio equipment of the Bf 109F-4 (FuG 7a) and was armed with an engine-mounted 20-mm Mauser MG 151 cannon with 200 rounds of ammunition and a pair of cowling mounted 7.9-mm MG 17 machine-guns with 500 rounds per gun. The G-1 was powered by the DB 605A-1 or DB 605B-1 and included provisions for mounting the GM 1 nitrous oxide power boost system, with the main tank and liquid oxygen bottles being located behind the cockpit.

One additional modification to the G-1 that was not present on the G-0 models included the fitting of a pair of small air scoops just aft of the propeller hub on both sides of the fuselage. These air scoops were to provide direct airstream cooling of the powerful DB 605A engine, which during prolonged ground operation (such as extended taxiing) had a tendency to overheat causing the nose-mounted oil tank to seep over the hot engine. Fires could

occur immediately, in which case shut-down solved the problem. In the air, where shut-down was not possible, the only solution was bailing out. In addition to the air scoops, the G-1 included an oil tank that was redesigned to allow for cooler operation and better sealing.

Sub-types of the G-1 variant during production included several *Ruestsaetze* and *Umruest-Bausatze* conversion kits.

G-1/U1 Evaluation aircraft incorporating a reversible-pitch Messerschmitt P-6 propeller. The propeller was to act like a thrust reverser on short field landings by redirecting airflow. Only a few of this model was delivered.

G-1/R3 Long range fighter with the addition of an under-fuselage rack for the fitting of a 300 l (66 Imp gal) auxiliary fuel drop tank.

G-1/R6 Fighter/interceptor with a pair of 20-mm MG 151 cannon in underwing gondolas assigned to the bomber attack role.

G-1/Trop. A specialized tropicalized version of the G-1 variant for use in North Africa. Because of continual over-heating problems with the engine-mounted cannon in the desert heat, this model also replaced the cowl-mounted 7.9-mm MG 17 machine-guns with a pair of 13-mm MG 131 machine-guns to provide greater firepower if malfunctioning of the nose cannon occurred. The aircraft also was fitted with the appropriate dust filters for the supercharger intake and radiator areas.

It should be noted here that the possibility of more than one conversion kit being added to an aircraft existed, and often became the rule as the war progressed. In most instances, however, the specified aircraft only carried a single designation. For example, a Bf 109G-1/R6 could have not only been fitted with the underwing MG 151 cannon, but could also have had an underfuselage bomb rack (fighter-bomber) or auxiliary fuel drop tank schackle (extended range fighter/interceptor) added.

Bf 109F-4/Trop

Oberleutnant Hans-Joachim Marseille as *Staffelkapitän* 3./JG 27 at Quotaifiya, North Africa, 15 September, 1942. Final rank/score: *Hauptmann*, 158 victories (all in the West).

Bf 109B

Spanish Nationalist air arm at Logroño, April, 1939. Transferred from 2./J 88 *Legion Condor*.

Bf 109E-4

Oberleutnat Helmut Wick as *Kommandeur* I/JG 2 at Mardyck, Belgium, 6 October, 1940. Final rank/score: *Major*, 56 victories.

Bf 109F-4/N Trop

Leutnant Werner Schroer, 2./JG 27, in North Africa, September, 1941. Final rank/score: *Major*, 114 victories.

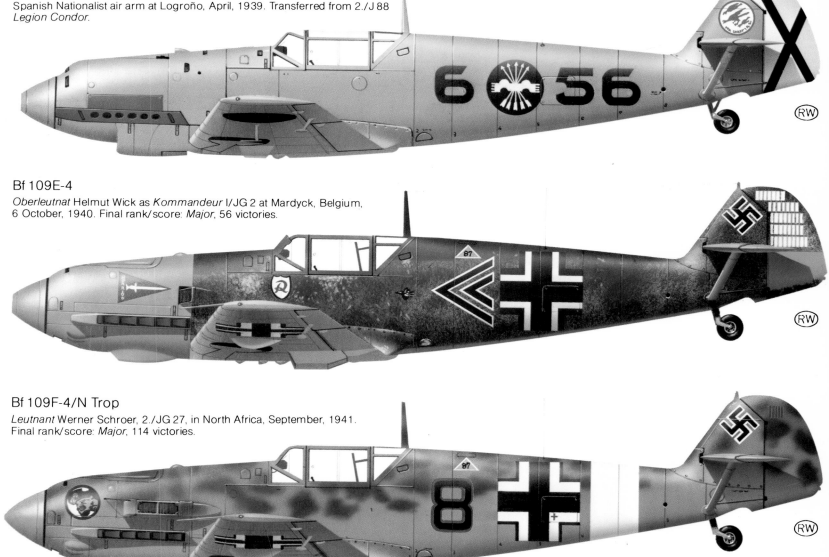

R. Watanabe

◀ Me 309A-1

As a new fighter concept the Me 309 series bore little relationship to either the Bf 109 or the Me 209 series. It contained many innovative systems but by 1943 it was clear that the Me 309 had little chance of gaining official acceptance. The 309A-1 was a projected model, a fighter with two MG 131s and one MK 108.

▼ Bf 109Z

Offering an expedient solution to meet operational demands, the 'Twin 109' was initially projected as a *Zerstörer* (109Z-1) and high-speed bomber based on Bf 109G-6 airframes. The concept was also adapted for the intended Bf 109 replacements resulting in the Me 409 (twin Me 209) and Me 609 (twin Me 309) projects, which also had promising long-range reconnaissance potential.

The first and only Bf 109Z prototype assembled from two Bf 109F-4 airframes was completed in 1943 but damaged in an Allied air raid and never flown.

Due to changed operational requirements all further development work was abandoned in 1944.

Bf 109Z-1 (data based on project estimates)

Span:	13.270 m (43 ft 6¼ in)	Weight empty:	6,000 kg (13,224 lb)
Length:	9.048 m (29 ft 8 in)	Weight loaded:	7,280 kg (16,050 lb)
Height:	2.690 m (8 ft 10 in)	Max range:	1,995 km (1,240 mls)
Wing area:	23.2 m² (249.72 sq. ft)		
Max speed:	743 km/h at 8.000 m (462 mph at 26,250 ft)		
Cruising speed:	570 km/h at 3,000 m (354 mph at 9,840 ft)		
Service ceiling:	11,700 m (38,385 ft)		
Armamant:	2×30 mm MK 108 mounted in engines		
	2×30 mm MK 108 in underwing gondolas		
	1×30 mm MK 103 off centreline in wing center section		

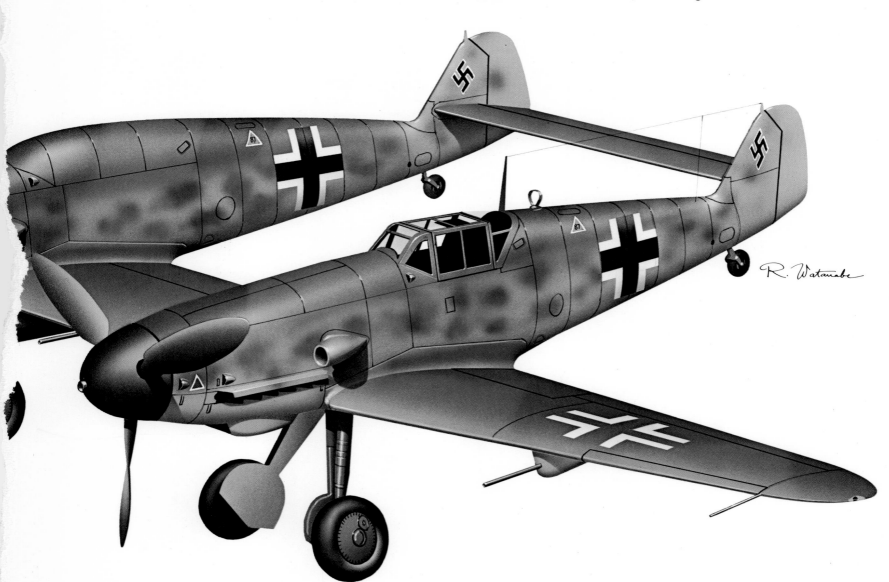

R. Watanabe

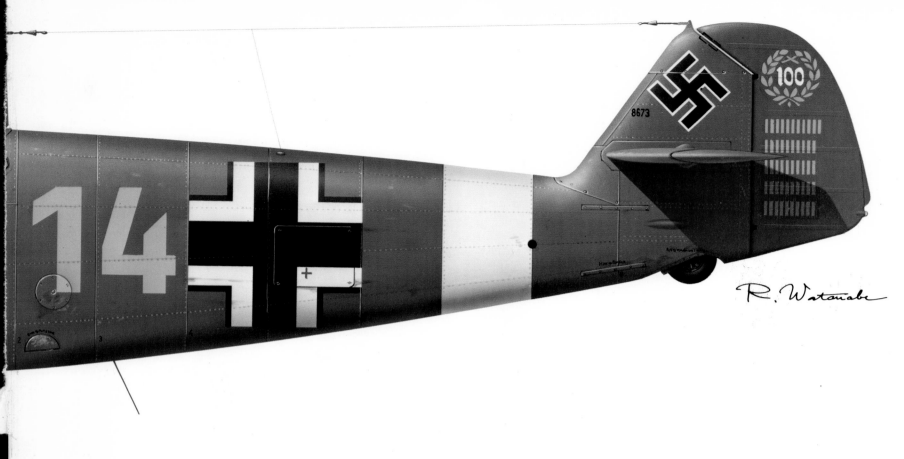

R. Watanabe

Bf 109F-2 'Special'

Oberst Adolf Galland as General of Fighters, December, 1941.
Final rank/score: *Generalleutnant*, 104 victories (all in the West).

Bf 109F-2

Oberstleutnant Werner Mölders as *Kommodore* JG 51, Eastern Front,
15 July, 1941. Final rank/score: *Oberst* (General of Fighters), 115 victories
(including 14 in Spain).

Bf 109F-2

Major Hannes Trautloft as *Kommodore* JG 54 at Siverskaya, Soviet Union,
winter 1941/42. Final rank/score: *Oberst*, 57 victories (including 4 in Spain).

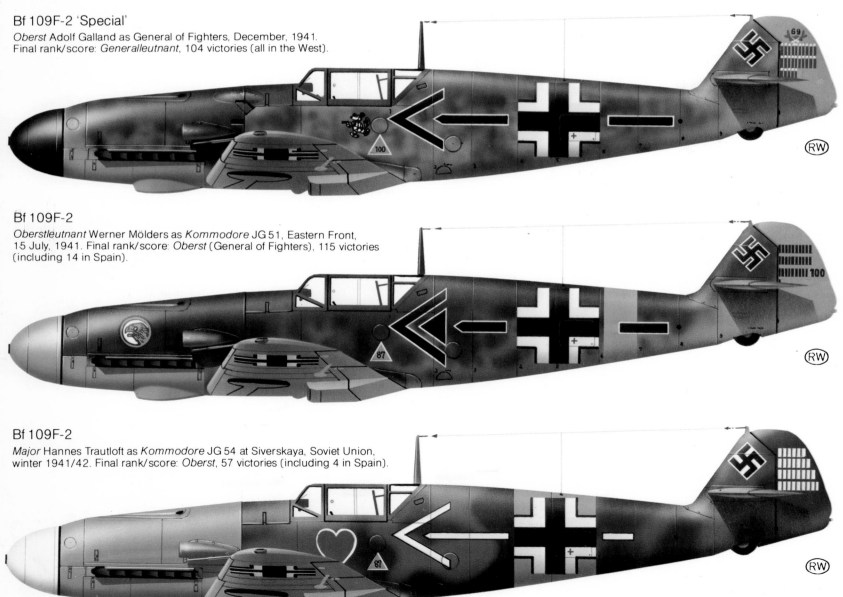

Bf 109F

Hauptmann Hans Philipp as *Kommandeur* I/JG 54 at Krasnogvardeisk,
Soviet Union, 31 March, 1942. Final rank/score: *Oberstleutnant*, 206 victories.

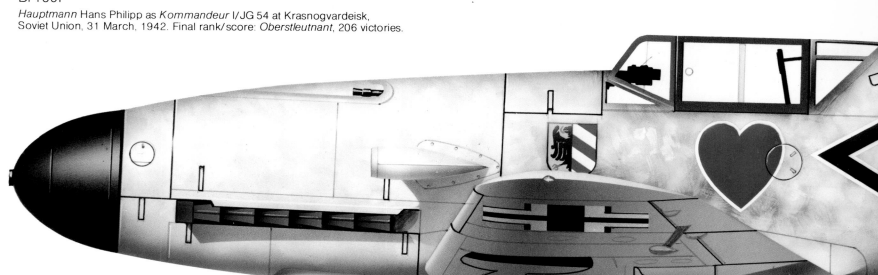

Bf 109F-4

Oberleutnant Siegfried Schnell as *Staffelkapitän* 9./JG 2 at Thêville, France,
late May, 1942. Final rank/score: *Major*, 93 victories.

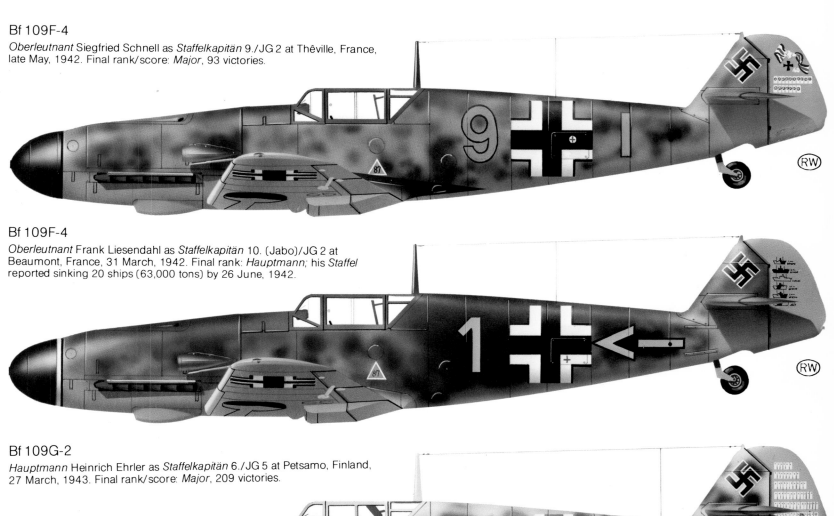

Bf 109F-4

Oberleutnant Frank Liesendahl as *Staffelkapitän* 10. (Jabo)/JG 2 at
Beaumont, France, 31 March, 1942. Final rank: *Hauptmann;* his *Staffel*
reported sinking 20 ships (63,000 tons) by 26 June, 1942.

Bf 109G-2

Hauptmann Heinrich Ehrler as *Staffelkapitän* 6./JG 5 at Petsamo, Finland,
27 March, 1943. Final rank/score: *Major*, 209 victories.

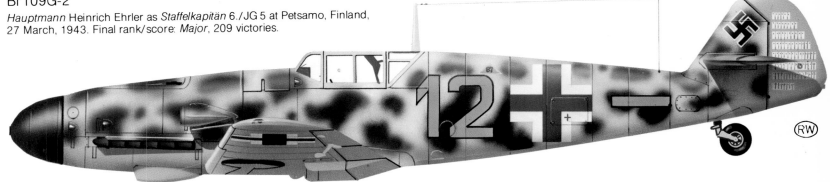

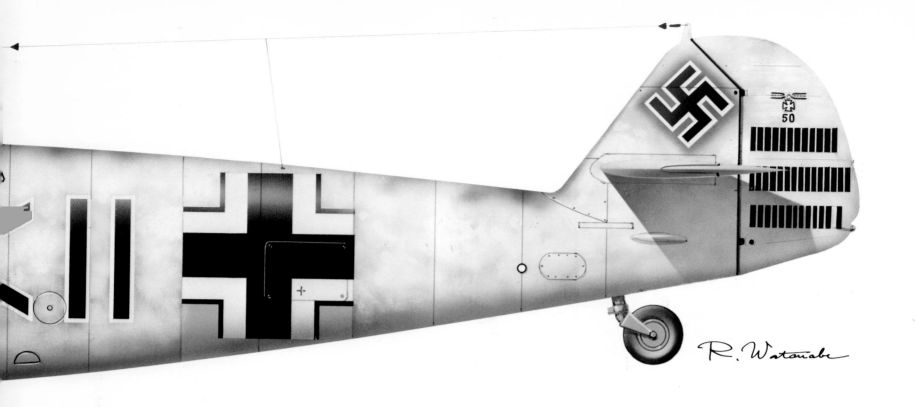

R. Watanabe

Bf 109G-2

Hauptmann Johannes Steinhoff as *Kommandeur* II/JG 52, Eastern Front, summer 1942. Final rank/score: *Oberst,* 176 victories.

Bf 109G-6

Leutnant Erich Hartmann of 9./JG 52 at Novo Zaporozhe, Soviet Union, summer 1942. Final rank/score: *Major,* 352 victories.

Bf 109K-4/R

Pilot unknown. I/JG 77, spring 1945.

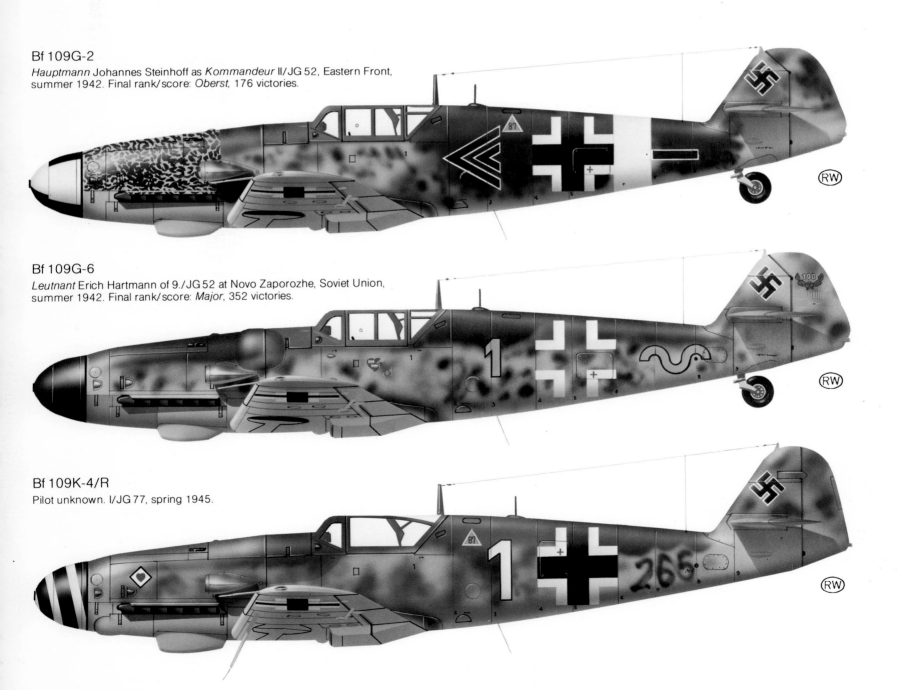

Produced in parallel with the Bf 109G-1, and in greater quantities, the Bf 109G-2 was identical except that it did not contain a pressurized cockpit or GM 1 power boost system. Sub-types of the basic Bf 109G-2 were also identical to those of the Bf 109G-1.

One unique experimental evaluation conducted on the Bf 109G-2 was a design for the development of an extended range fighter-bomber. A Bf 109G-0 (pre-production aircraft) was refitted with a DB 605A and redesignated Bf 109G-2/R1 for this test. The basic problem was in the size of the SC 500 bomb that was planned to be carried, in that it did not provide adequate clearance for takeoff when attached. To solve the problem, Fieseler designed an auxiliary single-wheel undercarriage component that could be attached to the underside of the fuselage just aft of the bomb, raising the aircraft off the ground. The undercarriage could be released after take-off through a series of explosive bolts and returned to the ground by parachute. To increase range, the plane was also fitted with two racks, or shackles for attachment of a pair of 300 l (66 Imp gal) drop tanks. After successful initial flight testing, however, the project was discontinued.

In April, 1942, the Bf 109G-4 was introduced into the assembly lines. The only major changes between it and the previous models were that it was not pressurized and had replaced the FuG 7a radio equipment with the newer and longer range FuG 16ZY equipment.

Although designated as a photo-reconnaissance fighter to be fitted with a camera installation in the aft fuselage, the Bf 109G-4 was delivered in several variants, and functioned in a number of additional roles for the Luftwaffe. In addition to the modified variants produced under the G-1 and G-2 designation, the G-4 also was ordered and/or delivered in the R1, R2, R4 and R7 models.

G-4/R1 Limited production fighter-bomber fitted with a ventral bomb rack for carrying a SC 250 bomb.

G-4/R2 Authorized fighter-bomber version incorporating the ETC 50/VIIId bomb rack capable of carrying four SC 50 bombs; however, this model was never delivered.

G-4/R4 Reconnaissance fighter incorporating an Rb 50/30 camera and a pair of wing mounted 300 l (66 Imp gal) drop tanks. This model, like the R2, never reached production.

G-4/R7 Standard fighter fitted with directional finding equipment installed inside the aft fuselage behind the cockpit, including a D/F loop antenna, to facilitate the locating of the aircraft in poor weather, poor visibility or after a crash landing.

With the introduction of the G-4 into service in August, 1943, the next version of the G-series to reach production status was the Bf 109G-3. This aircraft was nearly identical to the Bf 109G-4 in basic equipment, except that it incorporated the pressurized cockpit and GM 1 power boost system of the G-1 version and was designated for high altitude operation. Although relatively few Bf 109G-3s were delivered to Luftwaffe units, it was produced in a number of models including the R1, R2, R3, R6 and U2. The Bf 109G-3/U2 represented the first model of the Bf 109 series to use a non-strategic material in a major component. In this case, the tailplane was made of wood and a larger trim tab was included that was controllable from the cockpit. This aircraft was utilized for test and evaluation, with the wooden tailplane later being installed on several future G-series variants, except for the G-14 which utilized an entirely redesigned tailplane shape.

Bf 109G-6/R3, summer, 1944.

In addition, the Bf 109G-3 was the first G-series aircraft to exhibit wing surface bulges resulting from the use of larger tires necessitated by the increased weight of the G-series aircraft. The larger mainwheels, in addition to offering higher safety factors, required an increased area in the innerwing when retracted, and as the initial volume had been allocated to the smaller standard wheels of earlier variants, Messerschmitt either had to redesign the wing chord (which would mean complicated and extended testing), or add a slight drag-increasing bulge to the wing surface. The Bf 109G-5 entered production during the late June and early July of 1943, but did not appear with Luftwaffe units until January, 1944. The G-5 was powered by the DB 605A-1 engine, but in an effort to provide more efficient high altitude performance, was also delivered with an optional DB 605AS powerplant which was fitted with a larger supercharger. (Aircraft receiving the DB 605AS were designated with the letters AS after the variant, or *Ruestsaetze* (R), identification.) Armament of the Bf 109G-5 consisted of the engine mounted 20-mm MG 151 cannon and a pair of cowl-mounted 13-mm MG 131 machine-guns, which had been standardized for all future G-series variants. The increase in the size of the cowling weaponry resulted in still another set of external bulges, this time over the MG 131 breech blocks and ammunition feed chutes which were larger than those of the MG 17s.

The Bf 109G-5 was also fitted with a shorter radio mast and a directional finding loop antenna on later models, which incorporated the R7 directional transmitter inside the aft fuselage. One additional modification that was installed in the Bf 109G-5 was the improved vision "Galland" canopy which restructured the canopy braces and added bullet-resistant glass and thicker armor plate in key areas. This canopy was installed on a few late model G-5s, but did not become standard until the introduction of the G-14 variant.

Sub-type designations of the Bf 109G-5 to see service included the U2, R3, R6, R7, and the Trop., while authorization and plans for production of R1 and R2 models were received, but never started.

One unique modification incorporated into the G-5 was the addition of a pair of underwing Wfg. Gr. 210-mm mortar tubes for operations against Allied bomber streams. Designated as the Bf 109G-5/BR 21, the mortar tube concept was actually developed and flown initially on the Bf 109G-6 which preceded the G-5 variant in delivery to service units.

As noted above, the Bf 109G-6, although put into production at the same time as the Bf 109G-5, actually entered service first. It was identical to the G-5 variant except that it did not have provisions for cockpit pressurization. Produced in essentially the same models as previous G-series variants, the G-6 modifications also included the U2, U3, U4 and N designations. The Bf 109G-6/U3 identified the aircraft as being fitted with the MW 50 water-methanol supercharger boost system. Utilizing the tanks located behind the cockpit (used for the GM-1 system), the MW injectant, composed of 50% water and 50% methanol, was fed into the supercharger below the rated altitude of the powerplant to increase power through higher boost pressures. This system could increase take-off performance by over 300 hp, and provide similar power boosts up to altitudes of 6000 m (20,000 ft).

The Bf 109G-6/U4 was the result of continuing efforts by the RLM and Messerschmitt to increase the firepower of the Bf 109. The U4 modification incorporated an engine-mounted 30-mm MK 108 short barrel cannon in place of the 20-mm MG 151. Manufactured by Rheinmetall, the MK 108 had a rate of fire of 450 rounds per minute, was electrically actuated and automatically operated through a compressed air system separate from the weapon. Although a large number of G-6s were scheduled to receive the U4 modification, the limited supply of the MK 108s restricted its application and forced the retention of the MG 151 in most models.

The Bf 109G-6/N was a modification derived specifically for the night-fighting role. (As opposed to the use of the "N" designation in the E-series to identify use of the DB 601N.) The aircraft featured exhaust shields and flame dampers (to reduce the emission of light during night flying), the *Ruestsaetz* 6 (R6) conversion kit (which incorporated a pair of MG 151 cannon in underwing gondolas), and was fitted with the FuG 350 *Naxos* z electronic receiver. This receiver was capable of homing on the H2S radar used by the Royal Air Force pathfinder aircraft, allowing the Bf 109G-6/N not only to locate the Allied bomber stream without ground guidance, but also to vector other airborne Luftwaffe interceptor units to the target. For the installation of the FuG 350, a transparent hemispherical dome was fitted just aft of the cockpit and the D/F loop was relocated to the underside of the fuselage.

The Bf 109G-8, entering production in late 1943, was a photo-reconnaissance variant of the Bf 109G-6. Incorporating the use of either an Rb 12.5/7 or Rb 32/7 camera, the only other changes were in the deletion of the cowl-mounted MG 131 machine-guns to reduce the overall aircraft weight, and the addition of a port wing-mounted gun-camera. The incorporation of the wing-mounted gun-camera, actuated by the gun-trigger button, was done on an experimental basis to gather data for its installation in future Bf 109 variants.

By April, 1944, production of the Bf 109G-6 and G-8 had given way to the Bf 109G-10, which was intended to standardize several of the *Umruest-Bausatze* modifications, including the wooden tailplane, MW 50 power boost system, and semi-retractable tailwheel assembly. Because of the numerous assembly plants engaged in producing the Bf 109G, however, and the limited availability of several of the components as a result of continuous Allied raids against the supplying plants, a formalized standard Bf 109G-10 was never achieved.

The Bf 109G-10 was powered by the DB 605D engine coupled with the MW 50 power boost system and delivered an impressive 1,850 hp at take-off. The new powerplant had been fitted with a larger diameter supercharger and the compression ratio was increased by 15% through redesign of the cylinders. The cowl-mounted MG 131 machine-guns were retained and either an engine-mounted MK 108 or MG 151 cannon was incorporated, depending on supply. The G-10 also was fitted with the FuG 16ZY radio and FuG 25a IFF equipment, and a Revi 16B reflector gunsight replaced the previous Revi 12D.

Like other variants of the Bf 109G series, the Bf 109G-10 was delivered in various sub-types which incorporated a number of *Umruest-Bausatz* and *Ruestsaetze* conversions.

G-10/U2   Adaptation of the non-strategic wooden tailplane.

G-10/U4   Adaptation of U2 wooden tailplane and the addition of a redesigned and enlarged rudder, also fabricated as a wooden structure.

G-10/R1   Fighter-bomber adaptation with a ventral rack for carrying a single 250 kg (550 lb) SC 250 bomb or four 50 kg (110 lb) SC 50 bombs.

G-10/R3   Extended range fighter with adaptation of fuselage rack for attachment of 300 l (66 Imp gal) drop tank.

G-10/R5   Interceptor with addition of a pair of underwing gondolas carrying 30-mm MK 108 short barrel cannon.

G-10/R7   Although not designated as R7 due to more than one *Ruestsaetze* modification being used, the installation of the R7 location signal device saw wide usage on the G-10 series.   One of the more unique of the G-series variant was the Bf 109G-12 which was a two-seat training conversion of the basic Bf 109G airframe. Studies for this sub-type had been started with the Bf 109E version in 1940 (under the designation Bf 109S), but the concept had not been authorized until late 1942 when pilot training in the Bf 109 had been accelerated. For the prototype of this variant, a Bf 109G-5 was modified through removal of the pressurization equipment, and the incorporation of an elongated canopy with a second set of controls and pilot instruments. The canopy housing was hinged in the student's location, with the aft portion being curved outward to give the instructor a better view. A large number of G-5 and G-6 aircraft were converted to the G-12 variant during 1943 and 1944, although production of a G-12 straight from the assembly line never became a reality due to the pressing need for increased fighter strength and the limited availability of components. One *Ruestsatz* that was added to the G-12 variant was the R3, which provided the training flights with increased range and endurance through the installation of the 300 l (66 Imp gal) auxiliary fuel drop tank.

By July, 1944, still a further variant of the Bf 109G series was being delivered to the Luftwaffe, this being the Bf 109G-14. Utilizing the DB 605AS or DB 605AM powerplants, and standardized in the incorporation of the "Galland" type canopy first used on the G-5, the G-14 was armed with the pair of cowl-mounted MG 131 machine-guns and an engine-mounted 20-mm MG 151 cannon. Although only a limited number of this variant were produced due to the impending introduction of the Bf 109K, several modifications were adapted including the U4, U6, R1, R3, and R6. The U6 conversion was the installation of the longer barrel 30-mm MK 103 cannon as an engine-mounted weapon in place of the 20-mm MG 151.

The final production variant of the Bf 109G series was the G-16, which was essentially identical to the G-14 except that it reverted back to use of the DB 605D powerplant and had standardized installation of the R1 (ventral bomb or drop tank rack) and R6 (underwing mounted 20-mm MG 151 cannon in gondolas) at the factory.

Bf 109H *series*

The Bf 109H was the result of a proposal by Messerschmitt A.G. to the RLM to provide a high-performance high-altitude interceptor. The request from the German Air Ministry in early 1943 was based on the increasing need of

Revi C/12D reflex gunsight

the Luftwaffe for a fighter plane that could intercept and combat the Allied bombers at high altitudes, or use the advantage of altitude for escape or to surprise the enemy.

The *Hochleistungsjaeger* (High performance fighter) was proposed to be produced in two separate phases. First, an interim or temporary aircraft would be delivered to the Luftwaffe to provide capabilities during the design and development of the advanced, or second phase, fighter. The Bf 109H was proposed to serve as the interim aircraft.

The original Bf 109H was almost identical to the Bf 109F, utilizing the basic airframe, but had an extended center section of the wing which increased surface area for high altitude operation. However, changing RLM requirements during 1943, especially increases in operating altitudes, resulted in the abandonment of the original Bf 109H concept. Instead, an alternate Messerschmitt proposal was made to proceed on the Me 209-II programme which was to incorporate either a DB 628A or DB 603E powerplant. These engines were specifically developed with turbo-supercharger for high altitude operations.

Realizing that Messerschmitt could not deliver the Me 209-II before 1944, and recognizing the importance of receiving a new interceptor as soon as possible, the RLM instructed Messerschmitt to proceed with the basic Bf 109H program, but to modify the configuration to utilize several of the Me 209-II components, including the DB 628A engine. Due to the fact that a Bf 109G airframe had already been modified to accept a mock-up of the DB 628A powerplant as a prototype (Bf 109 V49) and proved the concept's feasibility for the Me 209-II project, a second Bf 109G airframe was diverted from the assembly line (designated Bf 109 V50) and installed with a development engine for flight testing.

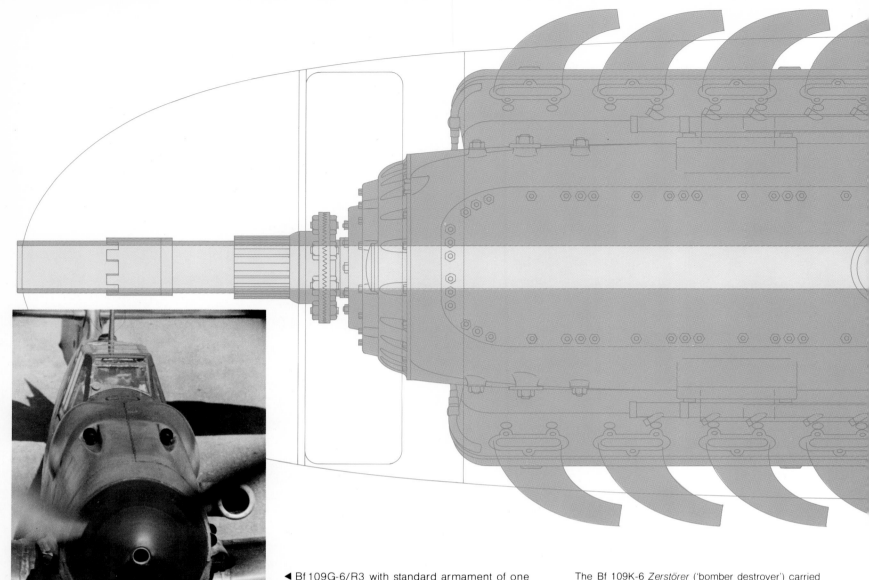

◀ Bf 109G-6/R3 with standard armament of one 20mm MG 151/20 through the propeller spinner and two 13mm MG 131 machine-guns with 300 rounds each over the engine. The MG 131 fired 930 rounds/min and had a muzzle velocity of 750 m/sec (2460 ft/sec).

(BUNDESARCHIV)

The Bf 109K-6 *Zerstörer* ('bomber destroyer') carried the exceptionally heavy armament of one 30 mm MK 108 or 103 in the engine, two synchronised 13 mm MG 131 machine-guns, and two 30 mm MK 108 cannon in the wings. Production began in January, 1945, but, only a limited number were ever used operationally. Heavy and unwieldy, the Bf 109K-6 was no match for Allied escort fighters.

Being nearly 180 kg (400 lbs) heavier and some 60 cm (2 ft) longer than the standard DB 605 powerplant used in the Bf 109G, the installation of the DB 628A into the Bf 109H prototype required the use of balance weights in the aft fuselage to insure maintaining of the aircraft center-of-gravity. This was to be compensated for in later models through the forward movement of the main wing attach points and an increase in the tail and rudder surfaces.

After initial flight trials at Augsburg, the V50 was transferred to Daimler-Benz for extended duration and altitude testing of the engine. While the testing of the V50 aircraft continued near Stuttgart, the Augsburg facility modified still another Bf 109G, under the designation Bf 109 V54, installing a DB 628 powerplant and incorporating the increased center wing section and tail surfaces.

In the meantime, while the testing of the new engine was being conducted at both Stuttgart and Augsburg, Messerschmitt initiated assembly of a number of modified Bf 109Fs under the designation Bf 109H-0 to conduct limit load tests of the widened undercarriage and increased surface areas. A number of Bf 109H-1s also were initiated and earmarked for delivery to the Luftwaffe for service evaluation. These aircraft utilized the DB 605A engine with the GM 1 injectant boost system.

The Bf 109H-1s were delivered to a Luftwaffe evaluation unit near Paris in early 1944, and while general handling characteristics were acceptable, the aircraft did exhibit a serious wing flutter in diving attitudes at high speed. To try and determine the cause and correction for the wing flutter, a number of Bf 109H-1s were returned to Augsburg for company testing and evaluation. During one of these tests, in April, 1944, the test pilot encountered the problem during a steep dive and pulled up sharply. In the pull-up the aircraft's wing was torn off. Limited testing continued on the aircraft; however, within the month, the Bf 109H program was cancelled and the RLM selected the Focke-Wulf Ta 152H for the high-altitude interceptor role.

Several additional proposals were offered by Messerschmitt based on the Bf 109H, including the H-2 (fitted with a Junkers Jumo 213E powerplant with GM 1 injection, engine-mounted 30-mm MK 103 cannon and a pair of wing-mounted 20-mm MG 151 cannon), the H-3 (fitted with the Jumo 213E engine and armed with a centre firing 30-mm MK 108 cannon and a pair of wing-mounted 13-mm

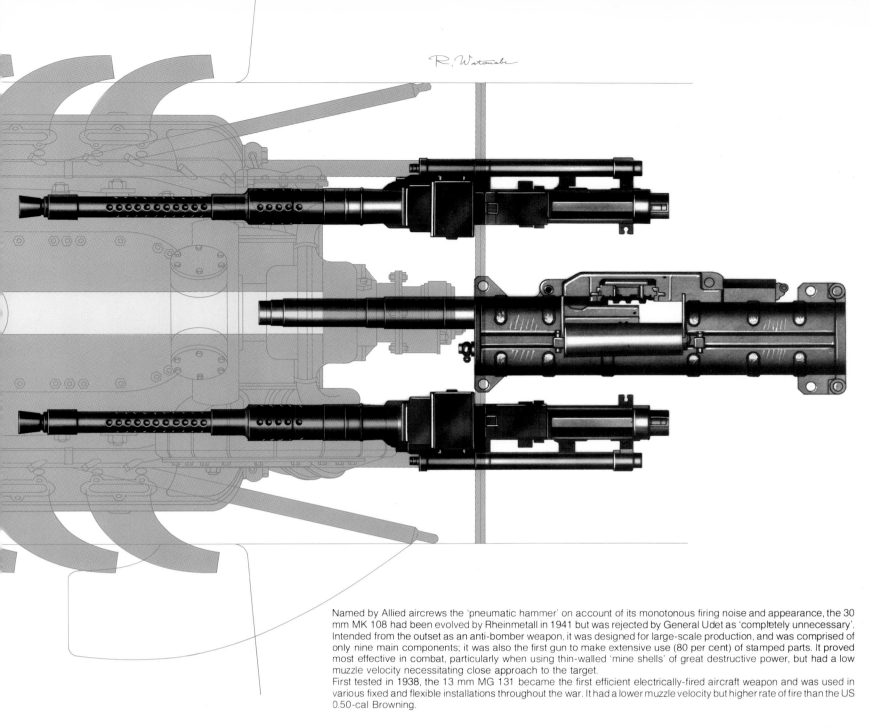

Named by Allied aircrews the 'pneumatic hammer' on account of its monotonous firing noise and appearance, the 30 mm MK 108 had been evolved by Rheinmetall in 1941 but was rejected by General Udet as 'completely unnecessary'. Intended from the outset as an anti-bomber weapon, it was designed for large-scale production, and was comprised of only nine main components; it was also the first gun to make extensive use (80 per cent) of stamped parts. It proved most effective in combat, particularly when using thin-walled 'mine shells' of great destructive power, but had a low muzzle velocity necessitating close approach to the target.
First tested in 1938, the 13 mm MG 131 became the first efficient electrically-fired aircraft weapon and was used in various fixed and flexible installations throughout the war. It had a lower muzzle velocity but higher rate of fire than the US 0.50-cal Browning.

MG 131 machine-guns), and the H-4 (reconnaissance aircraft with a camera installation in the aft fuselage). However, none of these proposals were ever accepted by the RLM for prototyping or development due to the success being enjoyed by both the FW 190D and Ta 152H.

Bf 109K *series*

The Bf 109K was the product of a standardization policy instituted by the RLM to reduce the number of variants and sub-types in the various basic airframes in use by the Luftwaffe. The plan was to select a basic variant, incorporating all the improvements that had evolved through the earlier sub-types, and establish a standard aircraft which would be manufactured by each of the aircraft plants involved in that particular design.

The Bf 109K was such an aircraft, and was based on the Bf 109G-10 variant, incorporating a number of the *Umruest-Bausatz* as well as several minor aerodynamic external features to improve streamlining. The pre-production aircraft, designated Bf 109K-0 for service evalu-

ation and acceptance, were similar to the late G-series production aircraft, but differed in that they had a raised cowling line just forward of the cockpit, a lengthened spinner, installation of the "Galland" type canopy, an enlarged tail assembly, and a fully retractable tailwheel which utilized a longer strut to raise the tail higher during take-offs and allow the pilot increased visibility in a forward attitude, and a modified rudder. In addition to the testing of the standardized G-10 armament of the nose-mounted 20-mm MG 151 cannon and cowling-mounted 13-mm MG 131 machine-guns, the K-0 prototypes also were evaluated with the incorporation of either a 30-mm MK 103 or an MK 108 nose-mounted cannon (the primary difference in the MK 103 and MK 108 was in the length of the barrel) and a pair of cowling-mounted 15-mm MG 151 machine-guns. The powerplant for the Bf 109K-0 was the DB 605B and included the installation of the GM 1 injectant boost system.

The initial production batch of K-series aircraft to be delivered consisted of both the Bf 109K-2 and the Bf 109K-4 models. Powered by either the DB 605 ASC or DB 605 DC engines rated at 2,000 hp for take-off and incorporating the GM 1 boost system, the K-2 and K-4 incorporated the

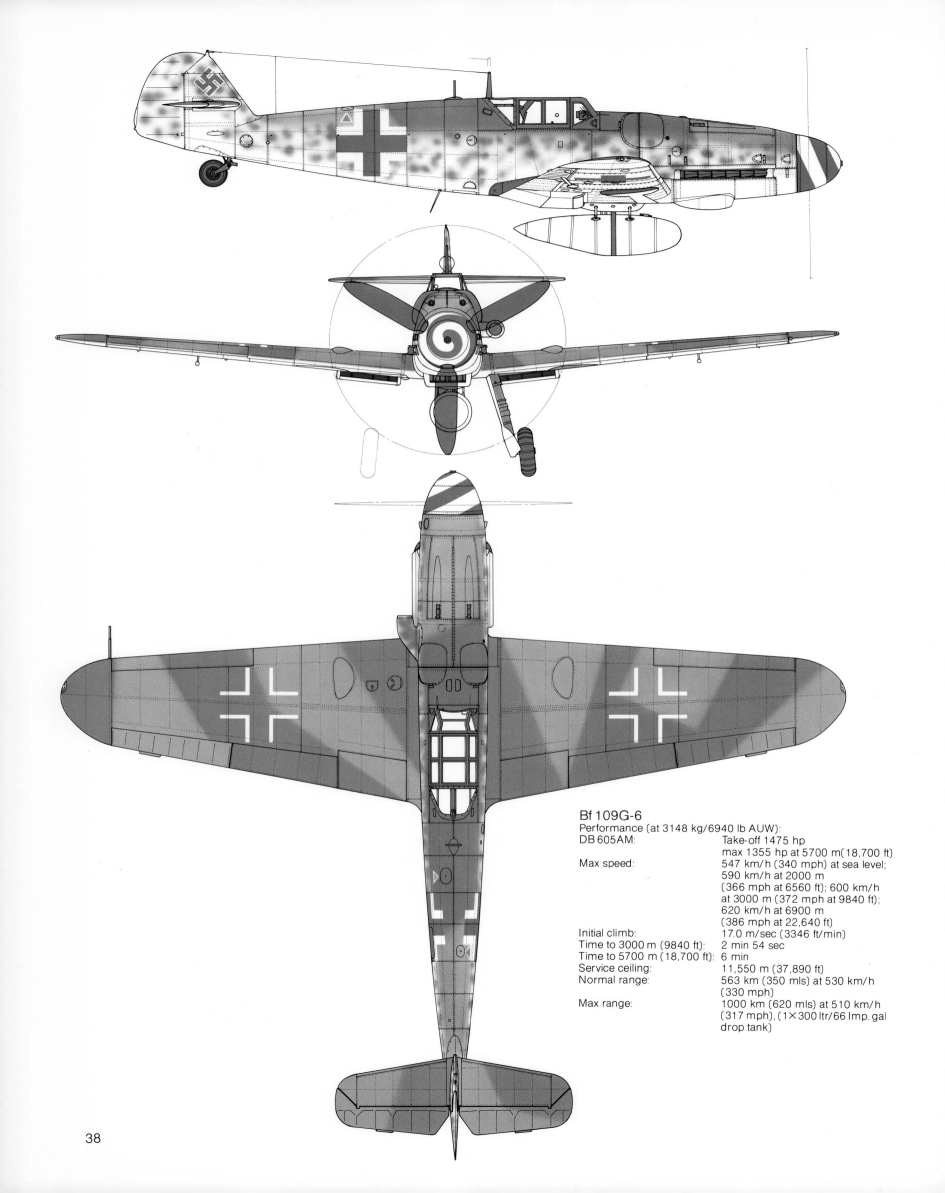

Bf 109G-6
Performance (at 3148 kg/6940 lb AUW):
DB 605AM: Take-off 1475 hp
max 1355 hp at 5700 m (18,700 ft)
Max speed: 547 km/h (340 mph) at sea level;
590 km/h at 2000 m
(366 mph at 6560 ft); 600 km/h
at 3000 m (372 mph at 9840 ft);
620 km/h at 6900 m
(386 mph at 22,640 ft)
Initial climb: 17.0 m/sec (3346 ft/min)
Time to 3000 m (9840 ft): 2 min 54 sec
Time to 5700 m (18,700 ft): 6 min
Service ceiling: 11,550 m (37,890 ft)
Normal range: 563 km (350 mls) at 530 km/h
(330 mph)
Max range: 1000 km (620 mls) at 510 km/h
(317 mph), (1×300 ltr/66 Imp. gal
drop tank)

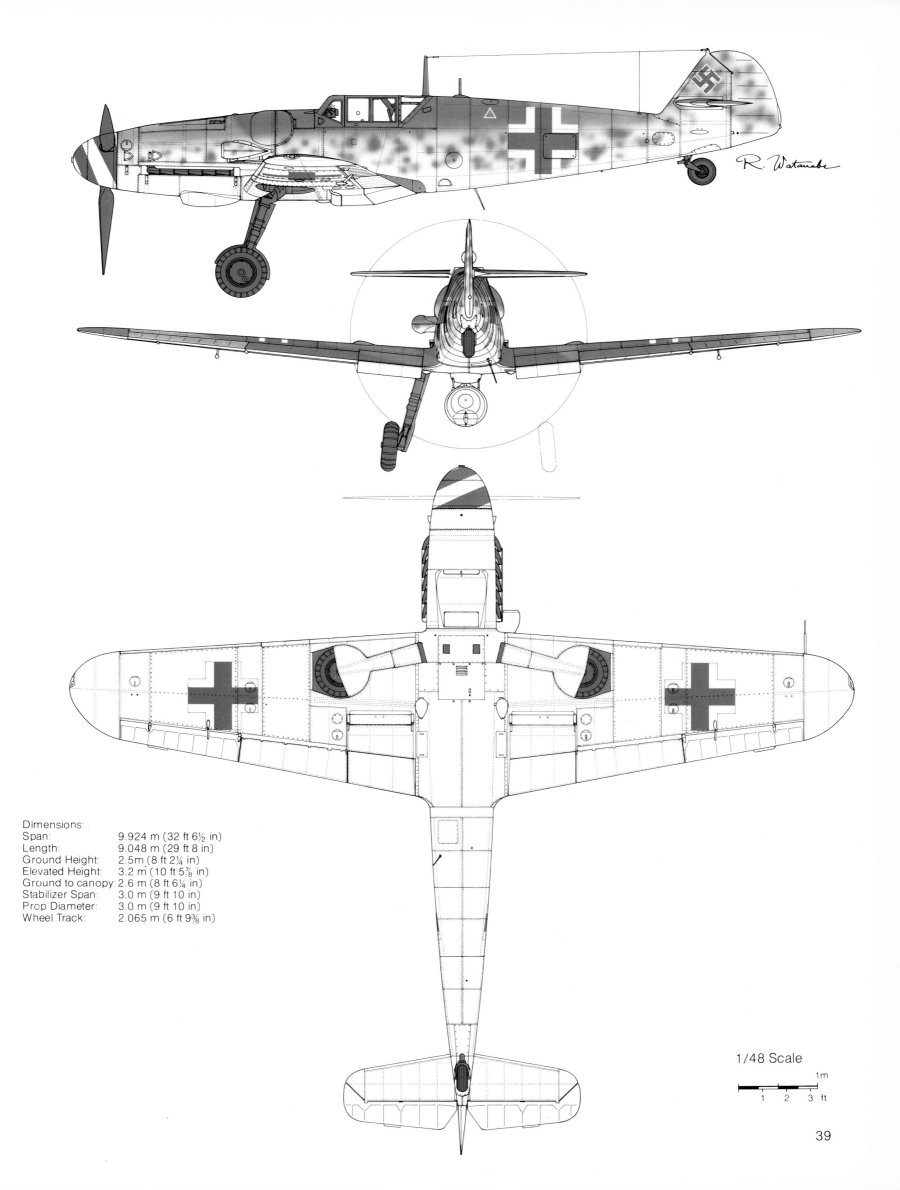

R. Watanabe

Dimensions:
Span: 9.924 m (32 ft 6½ in)
Length: 9.048 m (29 ft 8 in)
Ground Height: 2.5m (8 ft 2¼ in)
Elevated Height: 3.2 m (10 ft 5⅞ in)
Ground to canopy: 2.6 m (8 ft 6¼ in)
Stabilizer Span: 3.0 m (9 ft 10 in)
Prop Diameter: 3.0 m (9 ft 10 in)
Wheel Track: 2.065 m (6 ft 9⅜ in)

1/48 Scale

1m
1   2   3 ft

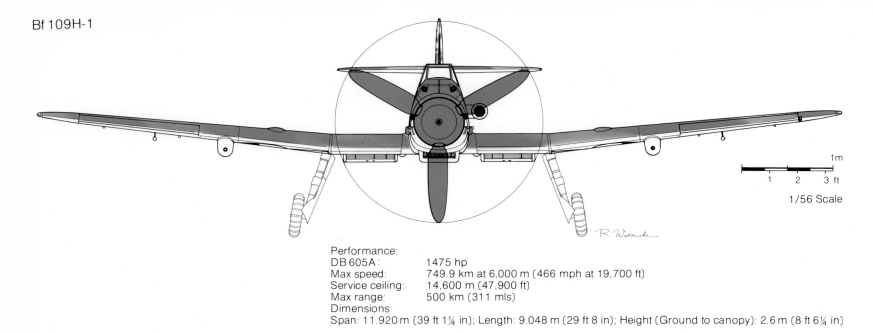

Performance:
DB 605A: 1475 hp
Max speed: 749.9 km at 6,000 m (466 mph at 19,700 ft)
Service ceiling: 14,600 m (47,900 ft)
Max range: 500 km (311 mls)
Dimensions:
Span: 11.920 m (39 ft 1¼ in); Length: 9.048 m (29 ft 8 in); Height (Ground to canopy): 2.6 m (8 ft 6¼ in)

modifications noted for the pre-production aircraft and standardized on the 30-mm nose cannon in combination with a pair of 15-mm MG 151 machine-guns. The only difference in the two models was in the installation of a pressurized cockpit into the K-4 model.

Ruestsaetze utilized on the Bf 109K-2 and K-4 models included the R1, R2, and R3 which provided the aircraft the capabilities of adapting to the fighter-bomber role with the use of the ETC racks (R1 and R2) or to the long range interceptor role with the R3 addition of the 300 l (66 Imp gal) ventraly-mounted drop tank.

With deliveries of the Bf 109K-2 and K-4 beginning in October, 1944, Messerschmitt undertook a further refinement of the basic K-series airframe to be used as a high-altitude bomber-interceptor. The designation assigned to this aircraft was Bf 109K-6. The aircraft was similar to the K-4, but reverted back to the 13-mm MG 131 fuselage mounted machine-guns and was fitted with a pair of 30-mm MK 108 cannons in the wings for added firepower, had a BSK 16 gun-camera installed inboard of the port wing cannon, and was equipped with a FuG 16ZY with underwing long range antenna on the port side.

A pair of *Ruestsaetze* were also available and utilized on the Bf 109K-6. These included the R3 (300 l (66 Imp gal) center mounted auxiliary fuel drop tank) and the R5 (30-mm MK 108 short barrel cannon in underwing gondolas). Both field conversions were rare and of an experimental nature due to the limited number of Bf 109K-6s delivered prior to the cessation of hostilities.

The Bf 109K-8 was produced as a photo-reconnaissance version of the K-6 variant, being fitted with a Rb 50/30 camera in the aft fuselage and fabricated without the fuselage mounted machine-guns, the cowling being faired over the gun troughs. These aircraft were scheduled to begin production during the early spring of 1945, however, with the end of the war, only a few of this variant ever left the assembly line.

The Bf 109K-10 variant represented a simple change in armament from the K-4 and the addition of one or more field conversions. Powered by the DB 601D engine, the K-10 was fitted with a pair of fuselage-mounted MG 131 machine-guns and a nose-mounted MK 103 cannon, and like the K-6 was fitted with a BSK gun camera and the FuG 16ZY

radio equipment. Conversion kits added to the few examples of this model to reach operational units included the auxiliary drop tank (R3), wing pylons for attachment of a pair of 300 l (66 Imp gal) jettisonable fuel tank (R4), and a pair of underwing 30-mm MK 108 short barrel cannon in gondolas (R5).

The final variant of the K-series to be produced was the Bf 109K-14 which reached operational Luftwaffe units during the last two weeks of the war. It was fitted with a DB 601L powerplant with a two-stage supercharger, offering over 1,700 hp at take-off with the use of 96 octane fuel. The obvious advantages of the new powerplant, which also made use of the MW 50 boost system, was that it could attain airspeeds of over 720 k/h (450 mph) at altitudes in excess of 10,700 m (35,000 ft).

The only drawback to the Bf 109K-14 was in its armament which, like on the K-8, was limited to a pair of fuselage-mounted MG 131 machine-guns and a single nose-mounted MK 103 or MK 108 cannon. Like the earlier models of the K-series, the K-14 also incorporated the D/F loop and FuG 16ZY antenna to supplement the normal radio mast behind the cockpit, and was fitted with the Revi 16B reflector gunsight.

Bf 109L *series*

Never intended as a Bf 109 variant, the Bf 109L was the result of the cancellation of the Me 209 program at the Messerschmitt plant at Augsburg. The Me 209 program had been initiated in 1943 with the proposal for the mating of the new Jumo 213E-1 powerplant with a Bf 109F-1 airframe. By the spring of 1944 the prototype, designated Me 209 V6 was ready for flight testing. However, because of the success and progress of the FW 190D and Ta 152H, the entire Me 209 program was halted.

Not willing to concede the production of the new high-performance high altitude fighter to Focke-Wulf, Messerschmitt decided to proceed with his project, changing the aircraft's designation to the Bf 109L. However, due to pressing production needs of the Bf 109G, and the work being conducted with the Bf 109H, no further efforts were expended on the Bf 109L.

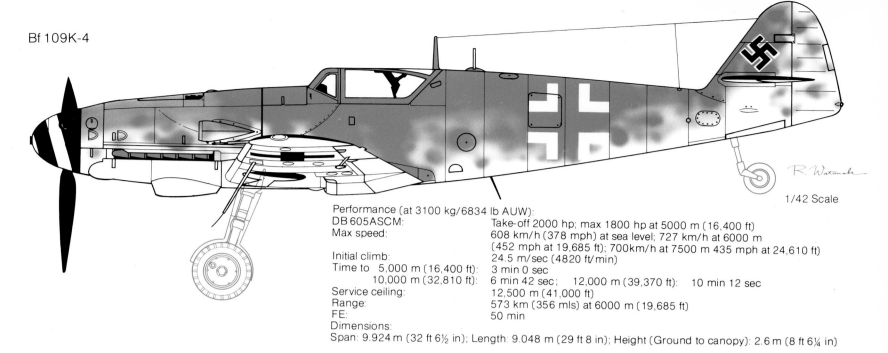

Bf 109K-4

Performance (at 3100 kg/6834 lb AUW):
DB 605ASCM: Take-off 2000 hp; max 1800 hp at 5000 m (16,400 ft)
Max speed: 608 km/h (378 mph) at sea level; 727 km/h at 6000 m
(452 mph at 19,685 ft); 700km/h at 7500 m 435 mph at 24,610 ft)
Initial climb: 24.5 m/sec (4820 ft/min)
Time to 5,000 m (16,400 ft): 3 min 0 sec
           10,000 m (32,810 ft): 6 min 42 sec;   12,000 m (39,370 ft):   10 min 12 sec
Service ceiling: 12,500 m (41,000 ft)
Range: 573 km (356 mls) at 6000 m (19,685 ft)
FE: 50 min
Dimensions:
Span: 9.924 m (32 ft 6½ in); Length: 9.048 m (29 ft 8 in); Height (Ground to canopy): 2.6 m (8 ft 6¼ in)

1/42 Scale

Bf 109S *series*

The Bf 109S was the designation that resulted from a Messerschmitt project to transform the Bf 109E into a two place trainer. No immediate need was forecast for its use by the RLM and the proposal was rejected. However, in 1942 the program was resurrected utilizing the G-series and culminated in the delivery of several of this model to Luftwaffe *Jagdgeschwader* and fighter-training schools.

Bf 109T *series*

Not unlike other countries which would eventually be involved in World War II, Germany realized the importance that sea warfare would play in deciding the outcome of any future conflict. Therefore, in 1935 the *Kriegsmarine* initiated the procurement of a pair of aircraft carriers under the designations, *Graf Zeppelin* and *Peter Strasser*. To provide air units for the pair of carriers, to be part of the German Fleet by 1944, a special unit of Bf 109Bs and Ju 87s was assigned to Kiel-Holtenau, a large harbor on the Baltic Sea, for training as part of the first *Traegergruppe* (Carrier Group). The initial training was conducted with specially modified He 50s at Travemuende where landings and take-offs were conducted at low speeds on an outlined landing surface to simulate the deck of the *Graf Zeppelin*.

Based on the initial success of the training operations, Messerschmitt was instructed to provide the *Kriegsmarine* with a carrier version of the Bf 109E. The design, designated Bf 109T (*Traeger*), was a simple modification of the basic Bf 109E-1 with an increased wing area, accomplished through the addition of approximately 60 cm (2 ft) to the outer panel length, the incorporation of an arrester hook just forward of the tailwheel, and the installation of catapult attach points and associated strengthening. The lengthened wings were also designed with a hinge to allow folding for storage which reduced the wing span of the plane to just over 4 m (13 ft), some 7 m (23 ft) less than the standard Bf 109E fighter.

The design was accepted by the *Kriegmarine;* however, because of the demand on production being con-

ducted at Augsburg, the program was transferred to Fieseler. Ten Bf 109E-1s were diverted from the assembly line as pre-production aircraft for the project and were given the designation Bf 109T-0.

Sixty Bf 109T-1's were also ordered from Fieseler. However, in April, 1940, work on the carrier *Graf Zeppelin* was suspended and finally in early 1943, was cancelled entirely. Fieseler was ordered to complete the order of 60 Bf 109T-1s, but to ensure their usability, they were to omit the carrier equipment such as catapult hooks and arrester gear. Stripped of the carrier equipment, the variant was redesignated the Bf 109T-2 and fitted with a ventrally-mounted rack that would accept either an expendable auxiliary fuel tank or a variety of bomb loads, including four 50 kg (110 lb) SC 50s or a single 250 kg (550 lb) SC 250.

The Bf 109T-2's deliveries started during March 1941 with the aircraft being assigned to units in Norway where operation from small airfields was a necessity. Being designed for carrier take-offs and incorporating the increased lift-producing wing surface made this variant especially suited to this mode of operation. This same short take-off and landing capability resulted in the few remaining Bf 109T-2s being transferred to the Heligoland fortress in 1943 as an island defense interceptor.

Bf 109Z *series*

Without question the most unique variant of the Bf 109 series was the Bf 109Z (*Zwilling,* or Siamese Twin). The concept for the aircraft had its origin in 1940 with the proposal for the joining together of a pair of He 111 bomber fuselages to provide enough power to tow the large Me 321 and Ju 322 attack gliders. The acceptance of this concept led Messerschmitt to initiate design drawings for the adaptation of a pair of Bf 109 fuselages joined in the center with a main wing and tailplane structure. The design was intended to offer the Luftwaffe a high performance fighter-bomber without the normal interference of already tooled production lines that would result with the introduction of a totally new aircraft design.

The Messerschmitt proposal was received with interest by the RLM and approval to proceed with prototype assembly and testing was received in early 1942. To determine the feasibility of the concept and to verify flight characteristics, a pair of Bf 109F airframes were mated to the *Zwilling* configuration late in the year. The only modifications to the fuselages was the incorporation of the structural members necessary to interface with the center main wing and tailplane sections and the relocation of the upper carriage. Each outer wing was also fitted with a pylon capable of carrying an SC 250 bomb and a rack with a load capacity of over 500 kg (1,000 lb) was added to the center wing section. Because of the use of the two DB 601E powerplants, an extra pair of underwing glycol radiators were fitted to the center wing section.

During the assembly efforts related to the prototype, Messerschmitt also initiated design work on an improved *Zwilling* configuration that utilized a pair of Bf 109G airframes and incorporated either the DB 605A (standard powerplant of the Bf 109G) or the Jumo 213E engine. Planned armament included a pair of engine-mounted 30-mm MK 108 cannon, a 30-mm MK 103 cannon fitted in the center wing section and an additional pair of 30-mm MK 108s in weapon gondolas attached under the outer wings.

The improved Bf 109G configuration was also designated to fill the fighter-bomber role through installation of a pair of ETC 250 bomb racks under the outer wings and the inclusion of a center section rack for carrying auxiliary fuel or bombs. In addition, the aircraft would remain a single-place design, with the starboard cockpit area being closed in and utilized for storage of fuel.

The initial prototype Bf 109Z was completed in mid-1943; however, during pre-flight trials, the aircraft was damaged in an Allied bombing raid on the airfield. Repair efforts were immediately instituted, but before they could be completed, the entire *Zwilling* concept was abandoned in favor of the new jet powered aircraft and the fighter-bomber variants of the Focke-Wulf 190.

Foreign Production and Service

While the Bf 109 series saw active combat service with several of Germany's allies during World War II, it was also purchased by neutral countries such as Switzerland, which utilized it as a peacekeeping aircraft during the conflict. The countries which fought alongside Germany and took delivery of the Bf 109 in variants from the E-series through the G-series included Bulgaria, Finland, Hungary, Italy, Rumania and Croatia. Not all of these aircraft were of German manufacture, however, as assembly plants in Hungary and Rumania were put into operation late in the war to bolster the declining production resulting from Allied bombing.

With the end of hostilities in Germany, the attributes of the Bf 109 were not to be forgotten, however, and two countries, recognizing the need for an interim fighter to fill the gap between their obsolete, or non-existent, fighters and the jet age, initiated their own production or modification program to the later model variants of the Bf 109. The first of these countries was Czechoslovakia, which in 1944 had been selected as a dispersal site for a Bf 109G assembly plant. The plant was fortunate in that at war's end, a number of components and sub-assemblies had been left behind by the retreating German forces. Thus, in 1945, the

Avia factory started production of re-engined versions of the Bf 109G-12 and Bf 109G-14 under the designations CS 199 and S 199. The new powerplant was the Jumo 211F which was available due to stockpiles of this bomber engine being stored in Czechoslovakia. These aircraft were produced until 1949 and served with Czechoslovakian units until the mid-1950's.

The S 199 was also purchased by the newly forming Israeli Air Force in 1948 as the Czechoslovakian government, in need of hard foreign currency, ignored the United Nations arms embargo in the Middle East. The S 199 served as a stopgap fighter until 1949 when agreements with the major powers were worked out, allowing Israel to purchase newly developed aircraft for its Self Defense Forces.

Spain, the country which had received several of the initial BF 109s and had inherited several early models after the Spanish Civil War, also produced postwar Bf 109s. Actually, production of the Hispano Aviación Bf 109 had been initiated in 1942 with the signing of an agreement between Germany and Spain for the license building of the Bf 109G-2. Under the agreement, Germany was to supply Spain with the components and sub-assemblies to be assembled in Seville. However, as the war progressed, the delivery of these components was delayed and arrival of the DB 605 powerplants never occurred. Unable to secure the engines, Hispano Aviación, still under obligation to supply the Spanish Air Force with the Bf 109G-2, substituted the Hispano-Suiza 12Z 89 12-cylinder engine rated at 1,300 hp.

The first of these aircraft, designated HA-1109, flew in March, 1945, with disappointing results due in part to the opposite rotation of the Hispano powerplant in contrast to the Daimler-Benz. The opposite rotation resulted in forces that had to be accounted for through unconventional rudder and aileron control and drastically reduced handling characteristics of the aircraft.

During the next two years numerous design and component modifications were made to the HA-1109 with it finally being accepted for service in 1952. In 1953, cancellation of production of the Hispano-Suiza 12Z 17 powerplant resulted in a decision to re-engine with the British Rolls-Royce Merlin 500-45, with the initial Merlin powered Hispano-built Bf 109 lifting off from San Pablo Airfield in 1954. In just under 30 years, the Bf 109 had come full circle. It had started its career powered by a Rolls-Royce Kestrel and had received its operational baptism in Spain. It was now powered by the Rolls-Royce Merlin and would serve with the Spanish Air Force until 1967, when the last remaining unit was phased out of service.

Detailed Construction

Designed to be simple and inexpensive and yet provide a strong, but not heavy, overall construction, the basic Bf 109 design remained essentially unchanged throughout its career, even with the many modifications incorporated for performance, armament and structural improvements. The aircraft was comprised of several sub-assemblies which were designed to be fabricated by a number of factories, or dispersal plants, for assembly at a common point. In this manner no one plant was depended upon for the entire program, nor could delays of schedule by a single supplier impact other plants. The exception to this was the Daimler-Benz powerplant, but because of the number of engine variants, no serious problems were incurred.

Envisioned for assembly in a manner like the American automobile industry, Messerschmitt designed his aircraft to consist of sub-assemblies with near complete internal components already mated, including hydraulic, electrical and fuel lines. Simple interfacing couplings and fasteners locked the mating parts together. This also simplified maintenance and made repair and replacement of Bf 109 components a short and easy task.

The Bf 109 wings were built around a single mainspar construction concept with flanges and reinforcement braces at all key structural or support interfaces. The mainspar was located in the center of the wing chord to provide undercarriage and wheel retraction clearance without interference. The wing had a flush-riveted stressed-skin of aluminum alloy, while the control surfaces were covered with fabric for light weight and responsiveness. The pair of wing panels, fabricated as individual units, but complete with all necessary control and feed lines, were joined at the fuselage centerline and attached to the lifting body at three points. The forward interface was comprised of a large steel forging which also housed the undercarriage struts and the base for the aft engine mount. The wing's trailing edge consisted of slotted flaps (inboard) and ailerons (outboard) which were hinged at the pivot points and attached to the wing through aft extending flanges. The leading edge slots had a maximum extension of 5 cm (2 in) on the outboard side and 7.5 cm (3 in) on the inboard side.

The tail assembly, which was mated to the fuselage just under the tailplane assembly and included the rudder, was built around a stringer and reinforcement structure similar to the main wing, with all non-moving surfaces covered with an aluminum alloy skin while the rudder and elevators were covered in fabric.

The fuselage was an elliptically shaped configuration with an all-metal support structure which consisted of longerons and radial, or vertical, reinforcing frames. The fuselage was fabricated in two halves and joined at the top and bottom with a flanged longitudinal joint which formed a Z-frame.

On the upper forward fuselage section, just over the Daimler-Benz powerplant, a flat structure for the mounting of the cowl machine-guns was provided. The guns were synchronized to fire through the propeller's arc.

The upper and lower cowling were both hinged and locked in place by a pair of toggle switches which were easily accessible for the ground crew, but sturdy enough to sustain high flight loads without failure. The opening of these toggles allowed both cowlings to be removed in a matter of seconds and provided direct access to the armament and powerplant.

The Bf 109 cockpit was also simple and uncluttered, making use of only essential instruments, but locating them in easily readable locations, with the Revi reflector gunsight situated off-center to the right on top of the forward panel dash and the ignition switch located on the far left corner.

The right, or starboard, side of the cockpit wall contained the primary electrical panel and warning lights mounted in the forward upper quadrant, while the oxygen hose and mask were located just under the panel and se-

cured in place with a pair of metal clips. The port side of the cockpit wall contained both the throttle and mixture control levers.

The flap and tailplane control was maintained through a pair of wheels just to the left of the pilot's seat with the vertical adjustment of the seat itself next to the wheels. The hinged canopy release was also located on the port side and was a simple mechanical lock which was pulled up and back to release the canopy seal.

Combat Operations

The Bf 109 was truly the backbone of the Luftwaffe during the war years. It performed in an operational status from 1936, when three developmental evaluation aircraft were sent to Spain to fight as part of *Jagdgruppe* 88, until the armistice of 8 May, 1945. It served in nearly every Luftwaffe *Jagdgeswader* as well as being the primary fighter for the air arms of Germany's axis allies. The only units it did not appear with were those specifically formed for a singular aircraft such as the famous JG 7 *Nowotny* which trained in, and entered combat with, the Me 262 twin-jet interceptor.

The Bf 109 achieved its first aerial victory of World War II on 4 September, 1939, only one day after war was declared between Germany and England. On this day, RAF Wellington bombers of No. 9 squadron attacked the German warships *Scharnhorst* and *Gneisenau* near Brunsbuettel on the North Sea. Unfortunately for the RAF, the Luftwaffe was expecting and prepared for the raid based on earlier attacks of 3 September. Bf 109Bs, Bf 109Cs and Bf 109Es of units based near Wilhelmshaven and Nordholz rose to meet the attack. In the encounter, two of the Wellingtons were destroyed by pilots of II *Gruppe* JG 77, the first losses of the war, and a further eight were destroyed by other fighter interceptor units and by fire from the German warships.

The initial recorded defeat for the Bf 109 occurred on 18 December when the RAF mounted still another heavy raid and reconnaissance mission over the German North Sea harbors in the Wilhelmshaven area. Again Luftwaffe units responded and destroyed a dozen of the intruding aircraft; however, a pair of Bf 109s were shot down. One of the Luftwaffe pilots who scored that day was *Leutnant* Johannes Steinhoff of 10 *Staffel* JG 26 who would go on to score 176 victories during the war and be given command of JG 7 in December, 1944.

For nearly a year, the Bf 109 ruled the skies over Europe, easily handling the RAF Hurricanes and early model Spitfires, the Curtiss Hawk 75s, Morane-Saulnier 406s and Dewoitine D.520s of the *Armée de l'Air* (French Air Force), and the various other obsolete fighters of the Belgium and Netherlands Air Forces. Its first real test came during the summer of 1940 when the Battle of Britain, one of the most important and decisive aerial confrontations of the conflict, at last vaulted the Bf 109 into worldwide attention and prominence.

For three months the Bf 109 found itself locked in a life and death struggle with its RAF counterparts for the right to air superiority over the English Channel and the British Isles themselves. The aircraft did everything asked of it and more. However, the distances from the bases in

France, and the continual utilization of the Bf 109 in an escort role, took its toll. Unprepared to perform in the long-range fighter escort function, its losses mounted. The Bf 109, in addition, suffered the disadvantage of fighting over enemy territory and when shot down, the pilots were unable to return to their bases to be assigned another aircraft as were their RAF counterparts. Finally, in September 1940, with heavy losses on both sides, the impending invasion of England was postponed and the beleaguered Bf 109 units in France took advantage of the time to reform and re-equip.

The experiences of these engagements over the British Isles resulted in the initial incorporation of the "U" and "R" conversions to the aircraft in an effort to compensate for its long-range deficiencies and to increase its multi-mission capabilities.

During the next few months, the Bf 109E continued to engage the enemy over the English Channel, in North Africa and in the Mediterranean, before it began to be phased out of service in early 1941 when the Bf 109F started transitioning into the Luftwaffe *Jagdgeschwader*. One of the first units to receive the new Bf 109s was JG 26 under *Oberst* Adolf Galland (later promoted to General and given command of the Luftwaffe Fighter Arm). It was Galland himself who scored one of the initial victories with the Bf 109F when on 1 April he was credited with a Supermarine Spitfire over the Southern English coast.

Two months later in June, 1941, Germany opened up a second front when it attacked the Soviet Union. The principal fighter during the early stages of "Operation Barbarossa" was the Bf 109F. The success of the first day alone can attest to the effectiveness, not only of the Bf 109, but of the Luftwaffe in general. Over 1,800 Soviet aircraft were destroyed on the ground and in the air for the loss of less than 50 German planes. Numerous Luftwaffe pilots were credited with five or more enemy planes shot down, among them Heinz Baer (final war-ending total of 220) and Werner Moelders (credited with 115 before his death in 1941 in a flying accident).

Another noteworthy Luftwaffe ace who piloted the Bf 109F was *Hauptmann* Hans-Joachim Marseille, who before his death on 30 September, 1942, accounted for 158 Allied aircraft destroyed. Flying his now-famous Bf 109F-4/Trop., "Yellow 14," Marseille had several multi-victory days including 6 June, 1942, when he claimed the destruction of six South African Air Force Curtiss P-40s.

In May, 1942, the Bf 109G began making its appearance with operational units in North Africa, France and the Russian-Crimea areas. By the end of the year it had virtually replaced the Bf 109F as the Luftwaffe's primary fighter aircraft. One of the first units to take delivery of the new variant was JG 52 based in Russia. The unit, which was credited with over 10,000 enemy aircraft during the war, had a pilot's roll that read like a "Wing of Aces." Among them were *Major* Gerhard Barkhorn (301 victories), *Major* Guenther Rall (275 victories), *Major* Wilhelm Batz (237 victories), *Oberst* Hermann Graf (212 victories), *Leutnant* Walter Wolfrum (137 victories), and *Oberst* Dietrich Hrabak (125 victories).

In August, 1942, a young replacement pilot was transferred to the unit. Assigned a Bf 109G as a member of the 7th *Staffel* of II *Gruppe*, this young pilot did not score until his 91st sortie. However, when he finally achieved his

30mm Ammunition: actual size

MK108 (A) Mine/tracer shell for air-to-air combat. Electric primer. Self-destructive. Fuze: ZZ1589A Muzzle velocity: 500m/sec (1640ft/sec)

(B) Incendiary shell for air-to-air combat. Electric primer. Self-destructive. Fuze: ZZ1589B. Muzzle velocity: 500m/sec (1640ft/sec)

MK103 (C) Tungsten-carbide core armour-piercing tracer, with additional incendiary effect, for use against heavy tanks. Not self-destructive. Muzzle velocity: 960m/sec (3150ft/sec), piercing 70mm armour plating at 60° up to 300m (984ft), 100mm armour plating at 90° up to 300m (984ft).

(D) Incendiary/tracer shell for air-to-air combat. Not self-destructive. Fuze: AZ1587 Muzzle velocity: 900m/sec (2950ft/sec)

(A)

Length: Overall, 205mm (8.07in); Shell, 144mm (5.67in); Cartridge, 91mm (3.58in)   Diameter of cartridge, 32.4mm (1.276in)

1. Fuze 2. Adaptor 3. Detonator 4. Booster 5. Paper disc 6. Explosive filler 7. Projectile body 8. Separator 9. Cover disc 10. Insert 11. Incendiary element 12. Closing plug

(B)

Length: Overall, 205mm (8.07in); Shell, 146mm (5.75in); Cartridge, 91mm (3.58in)   Diameter of cartridge, 32.5mm (1.28in)

Ⓡ Ⓦ

(C)

(D)

Length: Overall, 296.6mm (11.68in); Shell, 133.2mm (5.24in); Cartridge, 184mm (7.24in)   Diameter of cartridge, 39.5mm (1.56in)   Tungsten-carbide core, 85mm (7.24in) length, 16mm (90.63in) diameter

1. Fuze 2. Washer 3. Detonator 4. Projectile body 5. Incendiary element 6. Support ring 7. Rotating band 8. Equalizing body

Length: Overall, 298mm (11.73in); Shell, 144mm (5.67in); Cartridge, 184mm (7.24in)   Diameter of cartridge, 39.5mm (1.56in)

RW

initial victory in early 1943, it was only the beginning. By the end of the war, Erich Hartmann was to become the war's highest scoring ace with 352 aerial victories, all in the Bf 109G and K.

As previously noted throughout the description and discussions of the various Bf 109 variants, the plane was destined to fill many operational needs for the Luftwaffe. For the most part these were missions the basic aircraft was never designed for, and the required modifications usually detracted from its major advantages which included light weight and maneuverability. Among the more unique operational uses of the Bf 109 were the *Wilde Sau* (Wild Boar), the *Rammkommando* (Collision Commandos), and its attachment as a guiding aircraft to Ju 88s in the *Mistel* (flying bomb) configuration.

The *Wilde Sau* operations were the brainchild of *Major* Hajo Herrmann, who, during the summer of 1943 had proposed the use of single-place fighter aircraft in a night-fighter role over key German target areas where the enemy bomber stream would be illuminated by both searchlights and fires. The concept also had the advantage of visual contact, and was not dependent on the use of the *Himmelbett* line of FuG 220 *Lichtenstein* air-borne and *Wuerzburg* ground radar used by the Luftwaffe to guide its nightfighters to the incoming bombers.

With the advent of the use of chaff (small strips of aluminum foil dropped from the RAF pathfinder aircraft and bombers), the German radar systems became temporarily inoperative, providing only confusing readouts to the operators, not capable at that time of distinguishing contact with the metal strips from contact with the real aircraft. Until a number of modifications could be incorporated into the radar sets, *Wilde Sau* became the primary night-fighting weapon of the Luftwaffe.

In July, 1943, the decision was made to form an entire *Jagddivision*, with *Jagdgeschwader* 300 under Herrmann as the initial unit. Each of the new units, JG 300 near Bonn, JG 301 near Munich, and JG 302 near Berlin, were equipped with a single *Gruppe* of fighters modified with the incorporation of the underwing cannon or Wfr. Gr. 210-mm mortar tubes for increased firepower. Formed primarily around the heavily armored FW 190A, the limited availability of surplus aircraft forced each of the *Jagdgeschwader* to utilize the day fighters of other units operating from the same bases. This resulted in the use of several Bf 109G-6s in the new night-fighting role.

Even though victories by the *Wilde Sau* operations mounted, so did their losses. It became evident that although both the FW 190 and Bf 109G were highly effective in this new role, the increased weight of the added armament reduced speed and handling characteristics and made the landing of the aircraft extremely hazardous in inclement weather, especially at night. With the arrival of the late fall and early winter of 1943, the weather conditions and overuse of the aircraft became the major enemy of the *Wilde Sau* units. Equipment malfunctions, structural failures due to fatigue, and pilots bailing out rather than landing under potentially fatal conditions, rapidly reduced the number of available planes and the operations were cancelled in early 1944.

During this same time period, a new method of daylight bomber interception was authorized under the leadership of *Major* von Kornatski. The new tactic was designated *Rammkommando* and was based on the use of heavily armored FW 190A-8s which would attack the American bombers, getting as close as possible before opening fire. Although ramming of the bomber was not to be the primary objective, the suggestion was offered to the young pilots, who were instructed to bail out just prior to impact (a task more easily described than accomplished).

The success of the *Rammkommando* units lasted until late 1944 when the increase of Allied fighter escorts and the issuance of Allied Command orders to ignore the Bf 109G fighter cover and concentrate on the *Rammkommando* aircraft, spelled an end to this operation.

The use of the *Rammkommando* concept was revived, however, in April, 1945, when a special unit, *Rammkommando Elbe* was formed with Bf 109Gs. The special unit, composed of young volunteers inspired by patriotic conviction, flew only one mission. Over 80% of its aircraft never returned to base.

One of the strangest applications of the Bf 109 as an aerial weapon was in its use as the guidance plane for the *Mistel* or *Beethoven* flying bomb. The concept had been initiated in 1941, and revived in 1943 when Junkers proposed to the RLM that older Ju 88 airframes be loaded with high explosive and guided to a specified area by means of a fighter aircraft attached to the bomber by a center-mounted support structure which would be released near the target.

After a few successful tests with the Bf 109E, the prototypes were standardized utilizing a Ju 88A-4 and a Bf 109F-4, and production of the *Mistel* 1 began in May, 1944. The first unit to take delivery of the new *Mistel* system was *Kampfgeschwader* 101 which carried out its first *Mistel* operation in June. Although the success of the sorties flown by KG 101 was limited due to problems (among them, the aiming and releasing of the Ju 88), the potential of the concept was recognized, and further production was ordered which incorporated modifications in the support bracing and aiming instrumentation. The improved configuration was designated *Mistel* 2, and spelled the end of the Bf 109 participation in the *Mistel* project. The *Mistel* 2 and *Mistel* 3 were to utilize the FW 190A as the guidance aircraft. Aside from the operation of *Rammkommando Elbe* in April, 1945 (as described above), the last major operation of the Bf 109 in World War II occurred on New Year's Day, 1945. Under the code name "Operation Herrmann" the Luftwaffe mounted a major offensive against Allied airfields in France, Holland and Belgium. The plan was to surprise the Allied command with an all-out attack and destroy the bulk of continent-based Allied aircraft on the ground. With FW 190s and Bf 109s (including the use of the Bf 109K for the first time) the Luftwaffe force was composed of aircraft from nine separate *Jagdgeschwaders*. Claiming over 250 Allied aircraft destroyed, the Luftwaffe, however, suffered equally staggering losses and never fully recovered. The operational combat career of the Bf 109 was almost over.

Flying the Bf 109

Flying several variants of the Bf 109 for over seven years against almost every Allied aircraft, Herbert Kaiser, a Luftwaffe fighter pilot with 68 confirmed aerial victories, relates what it was like to pilot the Messerschmitt fighter and how it compared to its counterparts both on the Western and Eastern Fronts. As *Oberst* Kaiser describes it:

"The Bf 109B was not an easy aircraft to fly. It had to be directed with utmost attention from the split-second one gave it gas. The extremely narrow tracked undercarriage could not fully compensate for the normal tendency of the aircraft to pull to the right due to the prop torque. The maintaining of one's starting direction could be accomplished only by the smooth application of power, the balancing of the rudder, and the balancing of the elevators to lift the tail only after being airborne in order to keep constant aileron efficiency. Any casual disregard for those basic rules had a result of breaking the flight path and a possible crash.

"The cardinal rule during landing was that at the point of touchdown the gear and tail skid had to be oriented in the line of a projected roll without further attempt at directional control. Separation of aerodynamic lift due to insufficient approach speed, and excessive directional corrections performed during the landing procedure was the most common cause of crashes. The experienced pilot had these rules in his flesh and blood and this enabled him to make better use of his time by concentrating on other matters.

"Visibility from the cockpit was good, although during take-off it was quite restricted in the frontal area until the tail wheel left the ground. It was not at all reassuring to look forward and see only the large metal cowl, and this was why the aircraft had to be correctly oriented on take-off.

"Although the Bf 109B was useful as a frontline combat aircraft and far outclassed enemy aircraft of the time in speed and climbing ability, its initial Junkers-built engine was extremely sensitive and not sufficiently powerful.

"The Luftwaffe did not, in my estimation, have a truly superior and robust fighter aircraft until the appearance of the Bf 109E. The use of the DB 601 engine with 1200 hp, the increased speed, and the high climb rate made the Bf 109E, in relation to its counterparts, the best fighter of its time. Its armament of two machine guns and two cannon were more than enough to knock any enemy plane out of the air with a well placed burst of fire."

On 10 May, 1940, Kaiser, now flying as a part of III/JG 77, took part in the start of the Western Campaign against airfields in Holland and was credited with the destruction of two Dutch Fokker D.XXIs. He was then sent to France where he remained, flying patrol until the Dunkirk encirclement. Of these days Kaiser relates: "Although prior to the start of the Western Campaign in May, 1940, no German pilot could make a comprehensive comparison between British and French fighters and our Bf 109E, we firmly believed we had the best airplane based on comparative flying reports and an abundance of rumors. Personally, at the advent of hostilities, I had contact only with Dutch Fokker D.XIIs, and this fixed gear monoplane, approximately 80 km/h (50 mph) slower than a 109E, offered no particular challenge. Some of my comrades from neighboring units, however, had encountered the RAF Spitfires and Hurricanes, as well as the French Dewoitines and Morane Saulniers and thus affirmed what we all believed about our aircraft.

General Adolf Galland, commanded JG 26, one of the initial Luftwaffe units to take delivery of the Bf 109E. It was Galland himself, then an *Oberst,* who scored one of the first victories with the new fighter. He is now recognized by many aviation experts as one of the finest fighter pilots and tacticians of the war.

Oberst Erich Hartmann, known as the 'Ace of Aces' and the 'Blond Knight of Germany.' He ended the war as the world's highest scoring fighter ace, destroying 352 enemy aircraft. He did not join JG 53 until mid-1942 and remained with this unit throughout the war, flying various Bf 109 models, finishing in a Bf 109K. (ERICH HARTMANN COLLECTION)

Oberst Werner Moelders (left) and *Major* Hartmann Grasser (right) of JG 51. Moelders (115 victories) was later killed in a flying accident. Grasser (103 victories) survived the war. He served on Moelders' staff at JG 51 and was later assigned to JG 76. This photo was taken after both had safely returned from a mission over England. (GRASSER COLLECTION)

"In personally facing the RAF in the air over the Dunkirk encirclement, I found that the Bf 109E was faster, possessed a higher rate of climb, but was somewhat less maneuverable than the RAF fighters. Nevertheless, during the campaign, no Spitfire or Hurricane ever turned inside of my plane, and after the war the RAF admitted the loss of 450 Hurricanes during the Battle of France."

On 19 June, 1941, III/JG 77 was posted to Bacau on the Russian border and on the 22nd engaged in their first missions against the Soviet Air Force. Taking off at 0400 hours Kaiser achieved his initial kill over the Eastern Front later in the day near Balti. *Oberst* Kaiser recalls the Russian campaign: "Against the early Russian aircraft the Bf 109E was untouchable. The Soviet planes were slower and could not climb with us. They were, however, highly maneuverable, especially the I-15 and I-16, and one could not allow an encounter to deteriorate into a contest of turns. This was easily avoided, because we always had the element of surprise, due to our high speed and advanced communication systems.

"In Russia I encountered many varied aircraft, particularly bombers, for the most part the twin-engined Ilyushin DB-3, and later the Pe-2, and Il-2 attack bombers. The greatest losses for the Soviets, at least in our sector, occurred with the DB-3. A military version of a Soviet long distance record-breaker, it had great range, but was incredibly slow, and possessed poor defensive firepower. All weapons were hand-held, rifle-caliber guns and the bomber was blind to a direct tail-on approach. A single burst between the left engine and the fuselage into the wing root and the unprotected fuel tanks guaranteed immediate burning and unavoidable crash. It was considerably more difficult to attack the Pe-2 because of her speed, twin-tail assembly and the unrestricted tail gunner's vision.

"The Ilyushin Il-2 (Shturmovik) was also tough. A single engine fighter bomber not exceptionally fast, but very well armored, this plane required a detailed knowledge of its construction and a well-executed approach to destroy. The unforgettable Moelders showed me personally how one downed this aircraft. The Il-2 possessed armor behind the pilot; but just behind this armor was a small tank which was utilized as a starter cartridge. Totally unprotected and vulnerable, this tank was exploded with a single incendiary burst. Of course, in this mode of attack, a precise and accurate burst was necessary. Later the Soviets installed a rear gunner's position and armored the starter cartridge.

"During my participation in the Russian campaign, I also encountered the LaGG-3 and the MiG-3. I did destroy some of these, but it would be extremely difficult to make any well founded comparison with the Bf 109 because of my limited confrontation."

It was in North Africa that Kaiser received his first Bf 109G; "Here I was introduced to the Bf 109G which had an even more powerful engine than the F-model and a larger compressor (supercharger). It also had extremely good high-altitude performance. The air density of the North African sky was considerably less than that over Russia, and our performance could be maintained only through the constant use of the compressor. From a pure flying standpoint, the Bf 109G offered little over the Bf 109F. She was considerably heavier and still had the difficult take-off and landing qualities inherent with all the Bf 109 variants.

"During the African campaign, we were short of aircraft and for the young pilots with little actual air or combat experience, it was very difficult to master the 109. In addition, landings and take-offs were aggravated by the general condition of the desert air strips, not to mention sand and blowing grit. Because of these conditions, the relatively few number of airworthy planes were usually flown by the older, more experienced pilots, and the appearance of the same familiar names dominated the victory totals."

Describing the tactics employed by the Luftwaffe in North Africa in late 1942 and his impressions of some of the aircraft he faced, *Oberst* Kaiser relates:

"The classic dogfight was still partly used in Africa, and the lone sortie was prevalent. We were forced to this lone sortie tactic of surprise due to the overwhelming supply of Allied aircraft and, in this way, were able to spread ourselves over more area. Any other tactics would be coupled with high losses on our side, a condition we could not allow. Additionally, the speed and durability of the Bf 109G lent itself very well to this type of tactic. If we were overmatched, we could always break off.

"The Curtiss P-40 was not as fast as the Bf 109G and in a confrontation with this plane we had nothing to worry about as long as the basic rules of combat tactics were followed. We did, however, have to avoid getting into the middle of a large formation, for the P-40 turned well and as an old German saying goes, 'Too many dogs are the death of the rabbit.'

"The P-38 Lightning was equal to our Bf 109G in performance, far superior in range, and was a much more difficult adversary in a dogfight. However, I never employed any special evasive maneuvers when I encountered one of them. Evasive tactics, as far as I am concerned, were dictated by the situation and were a reflex reaction. For the most part, independent of the aircraft on your tail, one would utilize a steep turn and pull out to get behind his enemy, or pull up on the stick in a succession of stuttering steps to reduce speed, hoping the abrupt velocity decrease would not be picked up in time by the aircraft behind you, forcing him to fly over, exposing his belly. I always considered a turn-out and dive a' high risk tactic and, to my knowledge, this particular move was not used to any great extent by Luftwaffe fighter pilots."

In January, 1943, Kaiser was detached from JG 77 and sent to a replacement depot in Southern France as an instructor. He stayed there for four months before rejoining III/JG 77 and was posted to Italy where he destroyed four more aircraft. Then in January, 1944, Kaiser was returned to Germany for a routine medical checkup after which he was assigned to I/JG 1 under the command of *Oberst* Walter Oesau. With this unit he flew until 6 June, 1944, in the Defense of the Reich. From 6 June until 9 August he was stationed on the Normandy Front flying in a defensive role against the Allied invasion forces and describes his experiences as follows:

"Near the end of June, 1944, while attached to I/JG 1, on an airfield just outside Paris, France, an excellent example of the almost complete Allied air superiority occurred. I was vectored out to intercept an incoming flight of Allied bombers which was attacking our troops in the Normandy area. Our take-off had to be only in the smallest of groups (usually 2 to 4 aircraft) due to the Allied fighters which almost always waited above the bases for our fighters to emerge from cloud cover. We would be forced to sneak from our base into our target area by hedge-hopping over the terrain to take advantage of all the camouflage possible. Flying only a few feet off the ground kept us off radar screens, but sometimes put us on the side of a hill. We would only climb to any height when we had reached the attack point under the enemy planes.

"My flight of four aircraft sighted a formation of escorting Spitfires, and we positioned ourselves to engage them. We were instead caught by a second group of Allied fighters and in the process I lost my three men. Escape from the onslaught seemed impossible. Only because of my experience and the lucky appearance of a nearby cloud was I able to save myself.

"At this time the Luftwaffe was being ground into the earth. One could not count on his hand the days he expected to live. It was surprising to me that the Luftwaffe pilot had any nerve left at all, let alone the ability to prepare himself for combat with the enemy under these conditions."

Glossary

Abbreviations

		FuG	Airborne Radio or Radar Set	R	Field Conversion Kit Designation
		GM	Nitrous-Oxide Injectant	Rb	Automatic Camera
		JG	Luftwaffe Fighter Group	Revi	Reflector Sight
BFW	Bavarian Aircraft Works	KG	Luftwaffe Bomber Group	RLM	German Air Ministry
DB	Daimler-Benz	MG	Machine-gun	SC	Fragmentation Bomb
D/F	Directional Finder	MK	Machine Cannon	U	Factory Conversion Kit Designation
ETC	Electrically Operated Bomb Rack	MW	Methanol-Water Injectant	Wfr. Gr.	Rocket Grenade

Terms

Erprobungsgruppe	Experimental Test Unit	Jagdgruppe	Interceptor or fighter squadron
Flugzeugbau	Aircraft Builder	Kampfgeswader	Bomber Group
Flugzeugwerke	Aircraft Factory	Kriegsmarine	German Navy
Generalfeldmarschall	General Fieldmarshall	Major	Major
Geschwader	Three *Gruppen* (Approx. 120 aircraft)	Leutnant	2nd Lieutenant
		Lufthansa	German Airline
Gruppe	Squadron of three *Staffeln* (Approx. 36 aircraft)	Oberst	Colonel
		Staffel	Flight (Approx. 12 aircraft)
Jagdbomber	Fighter-bomber	Traeger	Aircraft Carrier
Jagddivision	Wing Composed of 3 or 4 Groups		
Jagdgeschwader	Interceptor or Fighter Group